CARDIFF AIRPORT
AT RHOOSE

CARDIFF AIRPORT

AT RHOOSE

70 YEARS OF AVIATION HISTORY

GEOFF JONES

To my mum in Pontypridd Road, Barry, who for years
has put up with my disappearance with the words:
'Just popping down to the airport.'

Front cover
Top photo: Concorde rotates from runway 30 on its last visit to Rhoose on 23 October 2003. (Kelvin Lumb)
Bottom photo: Aerial view of the terminal on 6 March 1976 during a French rugby airlift; clockwise around
the pier 3 x Caravelles, Comet IV, Vanguard, Caravelle, Boeing 727, Caravelle and BAC1-11. (Cardiff Airport)

Back cover
Catair's Lockheed L-1049G Super Constellation F-BGNG (an ex-Air France aircraft) was one of a trio that
flew to Rhoose in March 1970 carrying French rugby supporters. (Kelvin Lumb)

First published 2011

The History Press
The Mill, Brimscombe Port
Stroud, Gloucestershire, GL5 2QG
www.thehistorypress.co.uk

British Library Cataloguing in Publication Data.
A catalogue record for this book is available from the British Library.

ISBN 978 0 7524 5988 2

Typesetting and origination by The History Press
Printed in Great Britain

CONTENTS

Welsh rugby legend Gareth Edwards opens 'The Scrum Half' bar in the airport terminal building with airport director Albert Harrison on 26 November 1998. In 2011 this bar was rebranded as 'The Fly Half' bar. (Cardiff Airport)

FOREWORD

I remember with excitement my first flights, from Rhoose Airport of course. As a young Welsh rugby international most of our travelling to away matches had been by bus or train. It was in 1967 in a Cambrian Airways Viscount that I first flew. As a reserve with the Welsh team to Edinburgh in February and then, when I won my first cap, to Paris at the end of March. After that I flew from Rhoose on many occasions, as a member of The Blues, Cardiff RFC and of course as the Welsh team's No.9 and captain. This was in the days of the 'old' terminal building, on the south of the airport and close to Rhoose village, a cosy structure I remember, but with enough room for our enthusiastic band of players, officials and a few lucky supporters.

The long-gone days of 1971 were the career high point for myself and my Welsh team mates. We'd returned triumphant from the British Lions tour to New Zealand and had been summoned to meet the Prime Minister in Downing Street, London. Along with Welsh team mates John Dawes, Delme Thomas, Barry John, Arthur Lewis, Ray Hopkins, John Bevan and Derek Quinnell, plus the charismatic and influential Lions tour manager Carwyn James, we boarded a Cambrian Viscount at Rhoose for the short flight to London. What a day!

Since those heady days my family and I have been able to fly from Rhoose on business and for pleasure on many occasions, always thrilled to be able to use 'our local Welsh airport'. In 1998 I was delighted to be able to open the new Scrum-Half bar in the airport's terminal.

When Geoff Jones asked me to write the Foreword for his book about the history of the airport I wondered, 'why me?' Then I reflected on how many times the airport at Rhoose had played a part in my life and career. At the time I think I took the airport for granted, but on reflection, and looking at the magnificent and detailed history that Geoff has assembled here, I would like to pay tribute to his diligent work and encourage you to thumb and read its pages reflecting on the great national asset that we have in Cardiff Airport at Rhoose.

Gareth O. Edwards, CBE
Porthcawl, Wales
June 2011

ACKNOWLEDGEMENTS

Many people have inevitably helped with provision of memories, facts and pictures for inclusion in this book, and it is unfair to single out individuals from the following list; however, three have been particularly unselfish in providing a real pot-pourri of historical material: Malcolm Bradbury, Mike Freshney and Kelvin Lumb. Pictures have been credited as appropriate with the photographers names; all others are either my own or from my 'collection'. The contributors I wish to thank, in alphabetical order, are:

Peter Amos (A-B), Richard Baker, Adrian Balch, Dicky Bird (PFA and LAA), Malcolm Bradbury, Austin 'Aussie' Brown, Tony Carless, Mike Chard, Vince Cockett, Colin Dodds, Ken Ellis, Beryl Fitzjohn, Mike Freshney, Adam Gale (Aeros), Tony Harmsworth, Garry Hilliard (Cambrian Airways Society), Mike Hooks, Pat Horton (RAF Kirton-in-Lindsey and Hibaldstow Association), Cassie Houghton (TBI), Susie Johnson-Khalil ('Susie of Arabia'), Ivor Jones, George Keeble, Paul Keeble, Mike Kemp, John H. Lewis and Carl Bowen (both Pendyrus Male Choir, *Côr Meibion Pendyrus*), Kelvin Lumb, Barry Mahoney, Peter Marson, John Mead, 'Shelley' Michaud, Tony Merton-Jones, Peter Metherell Collection, Michael Ogden, Arthur W.J. Ord-Hume, Gordon Parsons, Martin Perkins, Peter Phillips, Eamon Power, David J. Smith, Keith Thomas, Robert C. 'Bob' Thursby, Chris Unitt, Ken Wakefield, Morley Williams, Nigel Williams and the LMLHS (Llantwit Major Local History Society).

TIME LINE OF MAJOR EVENTS AT RHOOSE

1942	RAF Rhoose officially opens on 7 April
1952	Aer Lingus operate the first scheduled passenger service to Dublin on 13 June
1954	Cambrian Air Services move their whole operation from Pengam Moors to Rhoose on 1 April as Cardiff's former airport is closed to commercial airline operations
1965	Glamorgan County Council take over responsibility for the airport from the Ministry of Civil Aviation and rename it Glamorgan (Rhoose) Airport
1970	Runway 13/31 (now 12/30) extension completed to a length of 7,000ft
	First jet airliner lands at Rhoose on 9 March, an Aer Lingus BAC1-11
1971	County Alderman George Adams lays the foundation stone for the new terminal on 31 March
	First transatlantic flight operated on 7 October by a chartered British Caledonian Boeing 707-399c flying to San Francisco via a fuel stop at Keflavik (Iceland)
1972	New terminal formally opened by HRH Prince Philip, Duke of Edinburgh on 11 December
1974	Airport taken over by a consortium of West, Mid and South Glamorgan county councils who rename it Cardiff-Wales Airport
1979	First charter flight to Toronto operated by CP Air Douglas DC-8s on 1 July
	Concorde makes its first visit on 21 October, a charter for Cwmbran Travel
1986	A further 750ft extension on the north-west end of runway 12/30 completed for operation of non-stop transatlantic west-bound flights – total runway length 7,725ft
	Annual passenger number total exceeded half a million for first time in December
1987	Starts trading as a public limited company, shares held by the three county councils and administered by a board of directors
1990	Air France becomes the first major international airline to launch weekday flights direct to Paris as total (schedule and charter) passenger numbers exceed 750,000
1991	Scheduled passenger numbers exceed 100,000 for first time
1993	Phase 2 of the terminal development completed for summer and officially opened by Lord Callaghan (a £2.7 million investment)
	British Airways BAMC airframe and engine maintenance facility opens in February
1995	TBI plc group of companies acquire the airport in early April from former local authority owners and start a £20 million investment programme. The airport is re-named Cardiff International Airport

2000   Charter passenger number exceed 1 million for the first time

2002   Sixtieth anniversary with British Regional Airlines offering over 190 weekly
                  scheduled flights to and from the airport

2003   Second fastest growing UK airport with 1.9 million passengers, split 52 per cent
                  charter and 48 per cent scheduled

2005   In January, Barcelona-based Abertis Infraestructuras SA acquire TBI plc

2006   The passenger total (charter and scheduled) exceeds 2 million and scheduled pas-
                  senger total exceeds 1 million for the first time

2010   Passenger numbers drop significantly (14 per cent) from 2009's total to 1.4 million
                  per annum due largely to bmibaby's reduction in capacity (approximately 200,000
                  passengers) and the volcanic ash cloud effects

2011   bmibaby announce their intention to withdraw all services in the autumn

INTRODUCTION

Cardiff's vibrant regional airport is an important gateway for air travellers coming to and from the principality. Cardiff Airport – Maes Awyr Caerdydd – is a focus and a microcosm of all aspects of Welsh life in the nation's capital and the principality as a whole. Currently handling around 1.5 million passengers a year, it is ranked approximately twentieth amongst UK commercial airports. Owned by the Spanish airports and motorway group Abertis Airports, who are ranked as one of the world's leading airport operators, with a strong presence in Europe and the Americas, the company has interests in thirty airports in nine countries, which handle more than 80 million passengers annually. The company manages British airport operator TBI, whose network of eight airports include Sanford (Orlando) Florida, El Alto (La Paz) Bolivia and London Luton. TBI first acquired the airport at Rhoose in 1995.

The year 2012 is the seventieth anniversary of the opening of the airport. That long-gone day on 7 April 1942 when the first RAF aircraft officially moved in at RAF Rhoose was not celebrated – it was part of the austerity and machinery of the Second World War when the Air Ministry requisitioned land between Rhoose and Penmark villages to establish a satellite aerodrome to RAF Llandow for training RAF Spitfire pilots. Rhoose may not have survived post-war, had Cardiff's accredited civil airport at Pengam Moors (2 miles to the south-east of the city centre) had land for expansion and not been prone to flooding, located as it was on low-lying land alongside the estuary of the River Rumney. Rhoose was dormant after the war until the Irish airline Aer Lingus was instrumental in its revival, wanting a suitable airport for a new scheduled Cardiff to Dublin service. On 13 June 1952 Douglas Dakota EI-ACE flew the first service, and Cardiff's 'new' airport at Rhoose started on the road to becoming Wales' premier international airport.

Several local government owners, many airlines, diverse charter operators and a burgeoning general aviation scene were all eclipsed by Rhoose's most significant operator, the 'national airline' Cambrian Airways. On 1 April 1954 all civil commercial flying had been transferred from Pengam to Rhoose, including Cambrian Airways, where they grew and grew. They were then assimilated into the national carrier British Airways and eventually disappeared in 1981. Cambrian represented for Rhoose not only the home-town major scheduled carrier, but a significant engineering base, a discipline that continues today with the huge BAMC (British Airways Maintenance Cardiff) facility.

Please note that despite the airport's many name changes, and recognising the current title 'Cardiff Airport – Maes Awyr Caerdydd', I will wherever feasible and appropriate refer to it as Rhoose. This is in no way a denigration of the status of the airport as the international gateway to Cardiff and Wales, but merely for simplification and consistency. My policy has been to use only photos actually taken at Rhoose, with one or two exceptions where the value of the illustration outweighs its location. Please also note that Rhoose's runway, now designated 12/30 (based on magnetic headings of 120° and the reciprocal 300°) used to be 13/31 (130°/310°) until the 1970s when due to the earth's magnetic drift, there was a slight variation resulting in this redesignation. I have used the runway heading designation appropriate to the era.

The diversity of airline operators and aircraft illustrated in this book amply demonstrates the importance of Cardiff Airport in a worldwide context. The number and variety of 'A-list' stars and personalities who have used the airport over the years helps confirm this importance, and in an economic sense illustrate how vital the world-class facilities at Rhoose are in relation to the economy of the area and the region.

1

WARTIME AND BEFORE: A NEW AIRFIELD IS BUILT

The bucolic **B4265** road meandered from Waycock Cross via Tredogan Cross westwards towards Fonmon Farm and East Aberthaw. It was known as Port Road, an important artery for trade long before the industrial revolution and the construction of the docks at Barry. The Port of Aberthaw was then the major port of call for shipping in the Vale of Glamorgan and this part of the Bristol Channel. Port Road completely bypassed Rhoose, a small, sleepy village then, apart from its cement works and railway station.

Aviation had barely touched the villages and communities of the Vale of Glamorgan. All commercial aviation activity was centred at Pengam Moors near Cardiff, the site of the city's municipal airport which opened in September 1931 initially as a field for club aircraft and private flying, and named Cardiff Airport from May 1934 onwards. Alan Cobham was touring Great Britain encouraging and advising on the establishment of municipal airfields. He landed at Splott Tidefields on 31 August 1929 in his DH.61 Giant Moth G-AAEV and stimulated Cardiff City Council into securing a site for a municipal aerodrome. By December 1929 Cardiff City Council had agreed in principle to the acquisition of 770 acres of ground at Splott, with the aerodrome clause being approved by parliament on 19 March 1930. This was further endorsed in the summer of 1930 with two flying visits from HRH the Prince of Wales, both times using a pair of Westland Wapiti 1A biplanes from No.24 (Communications) squadron RAF. A barnstormer from Berkshire Aviation Tours, Capt. Kingswell, also operated from Splott in May 1930. In July he was back in the Vale of Glamorgan at the Colcot Arms field in Barry giving joy rides in his Avro 504K. The following year a small club airfield was established at Wenvoe (close to the BBC television transmitter site), home of the Cardiff Flying Club. This operation started with the formation of Welsh Airways Ltd in January 1931 with joint managing directors P. Carpenter and T. Jenkins, who had the objective of establishing an aerodrome and flying club in the Cardiff area. They leased land from the Wenvoe Estate and later that year started flying from Wenvoe with three aircraft, G-EBYO an Avro 594 Avian IIIA and two Avro 504K's, G-ABGI and 'GJ. Nearby Barry was to hit the aviation headlines again when it witnessed one of Alan Cobham's travelling aerial circus visits on 26 September 1934, a field at Walters Farm, adjacent to the Port Road and just to the south of the present Tesco supermarket, being used for this significant aeronautical event.

From October 1933 and 1937 another aircraft was occasionally seen in the skies over Rhoose, Barry and further west. Mr Glyn O. Rees acquired the Civilian Coupé G-ABNT from an owner at Woodley, Berkshire, but then flew it to South Wales and the diminutive, high-wing, cabin monoplane was frequently seen flying from Pengam Moors, Cardiff. Now christened *Bunty*, he repositioned the aircraft to the Beach Hotel's garage at Pendine Sands from which he

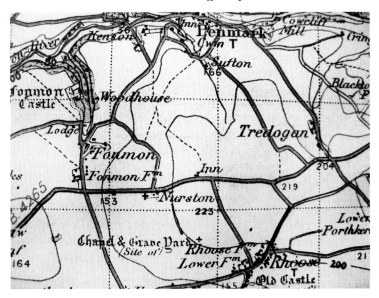

Pre-war map showing where RAF Rhoose was built. (Geoff Jones Collection)

flew the aircraft with his brother Dennis, visiting sandy beaches along the South Wales coast. In 1939 it was dismantled and put into storage in a warehouse in Carmarthen, the location of an auction on 9 February 1978 when it was acquired for restoration by Phillip Mann's Shipping & Airlines Ltd at Biggin Hill and from where it still occasionally flies.

The rumblings of war saw airfield construction move up a gear on the generally flat land of the Vale of Glamorgan. In 1937 614 Squadron was formed at RAF Llandow using Hawker Hinds and Hectors, but moved out to Pengam Moors in September 1939 – Llandow was bombed by a Junker Ju 88 on 6 August 1940 causing damage to a hangar on the main site. RAF St Athan opened in February 1939 as the home of No.4 School of Technical Training, quickly followed by No.19 MU (Maintenance Unit) in March as a civilian-manned aircraft storage unit. By January 1940 there were 280 aircraft on charge at St Athan, mainly Fairey Battles and Hawker Hurricanes. Slightly further west, RAF St Brides opened as a satellite to No.19 MU at St Athan in April 1941, initially with Hurricanes being stored here followed by Bristol Beaufighters and then Beauforts.

So why was RAF Rhoose built? When RAF Llandow was opened as an Aircraft Storage Unit (ASU) on 1 April 1940, it was called upon to host a training unit, a strategic decision in case of Luftwaffe attack, but also to free up airfields in the south-east of England for operational squadrons. Llandow was allocated No.53 Operational Training Unit (OTU) and needed a 'satellite' airfield nearby to share its workload. It was also reported that Rhoose would act as a decoy airfield, relieving pressure on Llandow in the event of a Luftwaffe attack.

Rhoose was built during 1941 and 1942 to operate as a 'satellite' to RAF Llandow, and despite being a long way from complete, was first used on 8 October 1941 by a Supermarine Spitfire I, K9933 from No.53 OTU, which had suffered engine failure and ended up doing a wheels-up belly landing on the rough ground. This aircraft set the historical aviation ball rolling at Rhoose, as the first aircraft, albeit ignominiously, to land there. It was also reported that RAF Rhoose, although not officially opened, was used unofficially by other Spitfires from No.53 OTU.

The official opening of RAF Rhoose was on 7 April 1942 when it came on charge with No.53 OTU, who remained there until 9 May 1943. Number 53 OTU had been formed at Heston (near London) on 18 February 1941 in 81 Group to train Spitfire pilots for Fighter Command squadrons using Supermarine Spitfires and Miles Masters. On 24 June 1941 'B' Flight moved to RAF Llandow followed by the main party on 1 July 1941, and hence to Rhoose in 1942. 'A' and 'C' Flights remained at Heston to form No.61 OTU. RAF Rhoose got off to an inauspicious start with five more minor accidents reported in the first week of operations, apparently because although officially opened, the airfield was still incomplete and the landing surfaces extremely 'rough'. Establishment of the unit was fifty-six Spitfires plus nineteen in reserve, seventeen Miles Masters plus five in reserve and four target-towing Boulton Paul Defiants with two in reserve – these Defiants were later replaced by Miles Martinets. Ivor Jones' book *Airfields & Landing Grounds of Wales – South* states that No.53 OTU at both Llandow and Rhoose lost more than ninety-two Spitfires, with fifty written off and unrepairable, fourteen damaged but repairable and eight ending up in the sea. Most of the accidents recorded off-airfield occurred in 1941 before Rhoose was officially opened, but certainly continued after April 1942.

Two 3,700ft-long hard runways were built in a cruciform shape, aligned 13/31 and 12/22, and with a perimeter taxiway linking the ends of these runways to form an almost square-shaped plan form. Alongside the northern and eastern taxiways several circular dispersals were also built for parking aircraft. At what stage the Nashcrete buildings and grass-covered, mounded bomb shelters were constructed on the south side of the airfield is not known. A watchtower was also built alongside the south-eastern taxiway and later four enlarged blister hangars were erected. Notwithstanding the infrastructure, it is to the eternal credit of Rhoose that the many hundreds of British, Canadian, Australian, New Zealand and Polish pilots did their combat and dog-fighting training in the skies of Glamorgan and over the Bristol Channel for nearly two years during the unit's tenancy of Rhoose.

The most significant improvement for the locals was the construction of a new, straight, concrete road from Model Farm on the old Port Road through Tredogan Cross to Rhoose village. This bypassed the airfield to the south-east, but the old Port Road remained in place within the airfield boundary, visible from the air for many decades to come. The Spitfires and Masters of No.53 OTU moved out from Rhoose to Kirton-in-Lindsey, Lincolnshire, in May 1943 and the airfield became almost disused for nine months.

RAF Rhoose's next bout of activity resulted from reconstruction work at No.7 Air Gunnery School's base (part of 25 Group) at RAF Stormy Down, necessary because the air gunners needed to familiarise themselves with night flying on a continuous basis; this couldn't be carried out at Stormy Down while remedial engineering works were being carried out to areas of the airfield that suffered from bad subsidence. On 7 February 1944 No.7 AGS moved in at RAF Rhoose with some of their Westland Lysanders, Avro Ansons (twenty-seven plus ten in reserve) and Miles Martinets (eighteen plus ten in reserve) and a reported fifty pilots. The Martinets towed sleeves or drogues, very much like wind socks, as targets, and the trainee gunners aboard the Ansons 'attacked' these targets. With the target tugs of anti-aircraft co-operation unit No.587 Squadron also using Rhoose as well there was apparently considerable congestion on the marshalling areas and taxiways during No.7 AGS occupancy of RAF Rhoose. Described at the time as 'a rudimentary airfield', it was necessary to position an airman at each aircraft wing tip whilst taxiing to prevent accidents. The only hangarage that was available at this time was four enlarged-over-blister structures erected alongside the dispersal pans alongside the northern perimeter taxiway. During No.7 AGS's tenure of Rhoose the infrastructure of the airfield was also improved from the basic 'cross' runway pattern with an extension of the 04/22 runway to the south-west towards Rhoose village. This reinforced concrete extension may not have been completed by the time that No.7 AGS returned to Stormy Down – the extension took the runway length from 3,700ft to 4,680ft, and provided the parallel peri-tracks, enabling the aircraft to move without impeding others landing and taking off. No improvements were made to the 13/31 runway. On 27 April 1944 six Ansons were added to the establishment at Rhoose bringing to twenty-seven the total of the type, with ten in reserve and two dual-control aircraft. The Martinet establishment was reduced to eighteen aircraft with ten in reserve and a few days later, on 1 May, three more Ansons from No.9 (o) AFU Penrhos arrived at Rhoose to complete the strength.

As with the Spitfires, there were many crashes and 'incidents' to No.7 AGS aircraft. Several Martinets experienced engine troubles and force landed or overshot the airfield. The worst day

for Rhoose and No.7 AGS though was Monday 8 May 1944 when a formation of three Ansons and one Martinet took off on a cine-gun exercise over the Bristol Channel off Southerndown and Porthcawl – Ansons LV300 and MG131 were involved in a mid-air collision about 1.5 miles off Porthcawl Point and plunged into the sea with the loss of all eight crew on board. Duty boats put to sea and found wreckage and an empty dinghy, but no survivors. The bodies were all recovered eventually and buried at Nottage. Number 7 AGS moved out from Rhoose and back to Stormy Down on 2 August 1944, Rhoose reverting to care and maintenance until it was transferred to 40 Group Maintenance Command on 1 November 1944 for storage purposes.

In total, four RAF units used Rhoose, but no squadrons, operational or otherwise, were ever based there. In May 1944 No.65 Gliding School, an Air Training Corps unit, was formed at Rhoose and was resident until at least March 1947; entirely speculatively, as no firm evidence seems to exist, the gliders are likely to have been early versions of the single-seat Slingsby T.7 Kirby Cadet (RAF Kirby Cadet T.X. Mk1) that first flew in 1936 and was adopted by the RAF during the Second World War for its air cadet training programme, 376 of the type being acquired. Slingsby T.21s may also have been used, the prototype of which first flew in 1944, a large, relatively heavy, open cockpit, side-by-side two-seater that would have been winch launched. Between 20 May 1946 and some time the following year 63 Group was also recorded as being at Rhoose until its disbandment, so although Rhoose closed as an RAF airfield in 1945, it continued as an active military establishment.

Post-war, RAF Rhoose quickly fell into an unserviceable condition. One Bridgend resident I talked to remembers the airfield being used post-war for the storage of surplus Second World War bombs before they were taken to sea and dumped in the deep water of the western approaches of the Bristol Channel. The stockpiles of bombs could be seen from the footpath – still very much in existence – that skirted the western fringes of the airfield alongside the old runway 12/22 and which was accessed from the old Port Road near the Carpenters Arms public house. This is now the Highwayman Inn and used as well as an off-airport, long-stay car park. This storage facility was under No.59 Maintenance Unit (59 MU) which had been formed in May 1941 in 42 Group as the Air Ammunition Park, later as the explosives storage unit and finally as the ammunition depot at Newland, near Coleford in Gloucestershire. Rhoose became a 'detached site' to Newland on 6 June 1945 and they formally moved in on 15 April 1946, and were not disbanded until 29 February 1952, although with the disbanding of No.59 MU, the airfield is thought to have closed as an active site around January 1948. As well as the small watch office and a few hangars, Rhoose had accumulated many neighbouring domestic sites: airmen's, sergeants' and officers' sleeping accommodations were on the south side of the road leading in to Rhoose village, with the WAAF's accommodation separated on the airfield side of the road. There was also a communal mess and sick quarters which fell into disrepair.

Opposite from top

Taken in June 1942, this Spitfire 1A AR214 was one of those operational at RAF Rhoose with 53 OTU – 'OB' and 'KU' codes were allocated to No.53 OTU, with the third letter the aircraft's individual code. (Zdenek Hurt via David J. Smith)

A 53 OTU Spitfire 1A has its roundels repainted at RAF Rhoose during summer 1942 by Polish airmen who were stationed there – the Air Ministry decreed that the change from A1 to C1 roundels had to be completed by July 1942 so these airmen are probably rushing to complete their task. (Zdenek Hurt via David J. Smith)

Miles Martinet TT.1 of No.7 AGS operating from RAF Rhoose, seen above the Satellite Landing Ground at St Bride's. (Mike Kemp Collection)

This wartime Nashcrete building was refurbished post-war and used by Cambrian Airways as their air-freight building. (Cardiff Airport)

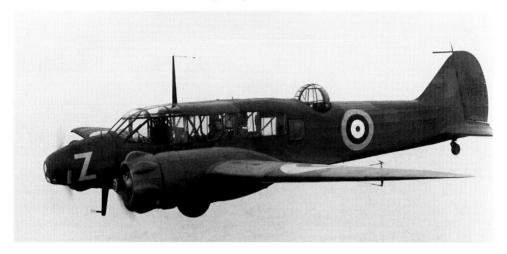

L7958 Avro Anson, similar to those operated from Rhoose in 1944 by 7 Air Gunnery School. (Via Tony Harmsworth)

Development of the former RAF Rhoose may not have happened at all had an ambitious plan by the South Wales Civil Air Base Committee come to fruition. This was in 1944 when thoughts were turning to post-war peace. The *Western Mail* for 18 March 1944 reported a conference representing local authorities and the Welsh Parliamentary Party in Cardiff that day to discuss proposals to establish an international airport for South Wales post-war with six sites under consideration. These were at Llanwern, Rhoose, Llantwit Major, Fairwood Common, Pembrey and St David's. The report concludes: 'only two sites would comply closely with the Ministry's specification, Llantwit Major and St. Davids. The favourable geographical situation of South Wales for a suggested base is emphasised, because it is in direct line east of New York.' A further report was commissioned from E. John Powell, the Glamorgan county engineer and surveyor for construction of this new international airport in the Vale of Glamorgan. The report was presented to the committee in 1945 and was based on the supposition that transatlantic flights would need alternative airports to London in case of bad weather diversions or other problems and that these be on the western fringes of the UK. Prestwick in Scotland – already in existence – was one location, but a site near Llantwit Major in the Vale of Glamorgan was proposed as another. The site proposed straddled the railway line from Llantwit to Bridgend, and road access was also considered good – it embraced part of the RAF Llandow site. Three runways were proposed, a huge 15,000ft runway 09/27 (east/west), plus a 12,000ft runway 12/22 north-east to south-west) and an 11,550ft runway 13/31 (north-west to south-east). Terminal buildings were not in the remit of the report, but a curved, Berlin Templehof-style facility with 'awning' extending over parked airliners was mentioned, plus the many other facilities related to a 'modern' international airport. This ambitiously innovative idea came to nought. In 1947 plans were also mooted to start regular scheduled services between the UK and South America from RAF Llandow, but this proposal also came to nothing. Unsuspected at the time, but the failure of these proposals probably helped considerably in the promotion of Rhoose when an alternative site for Cardiff's airport was on the agenda.

2

AER LINGUS AND THE IRISH CONNECTION

The Irish national airline, founded as Aer Lingus Teoranta in May 1936, had been flying scheduled services with its de Havilland Dragon from its base at Baldonnel near Dublin to Bristol (Whitchurch) and onwards to London (Croydon) for much of the pre-war period. Post-war, initially with a fleet of Vickers Vikings supplemented with Douglas Dakotas, Aer Lingus services from Dublin to Liverpool, Manchester, Belfast and Glasgow were inaugurated, as well as to several European capitals. It was the airline's desire to add scheduled services to the Welsh capital that caused Aer Lingus to look at an alternative to the small and often unserviceable Cardiff Airport at Pengam Moors. The former RAF field at Rhoose, although 13 miles from Cardiff city centre, was considered and assessed as a fairly easy task to bring up to serviceability again, plus it had the huge benefit of 4,680ft and 3700ft hard, all-weather runways which Pengam Moors did not. There was little else at Rhoose, though; several ex-wartime Nashcrete concrete buildings, a watchtower and taxiways (or peri-tracks) about summed up Rhoose's infrastructure.

The Irish Times newspaper announced on 10 April 1952 that Aer Lingus was to start a Dublin to Cardiff scheduled service on 13 June, the first Aer Lingus scheduled service to Wales. They also announced that the airline would operate to Rhoose Airport, the former RAF station. The year 1952 saw Aer Lingus commence scheduled services from Dublin to both Edinburgh and Cardiff, the first one opening on 22 April and the new Cardiff service on 13 June as planned. Both were inaugurated by Dakota EI-ACE, and on the first flight from Dublin the Lord Mayor of Dublin arrived and was promptly driven to Dyffryn House for a celebratory lunch. The *Western Mail* reported that the return flight from Rhoose to Dublin took sixty-five minutes. Cardiff's airport at Rhoose had started its long and illustrious career as a civilian airport.

The Edinburgh service proved to be the more successful of the two new Aer Lingus services, with strong demand requiring the operation of extra services during July and August. While results on the Dublin to Rhoose service were not as good, they nonetheless justified retention of the route in Aer Lingus's winter schedule. For winter 1952/53 Rhoose was served as an en route stop on the Dublin to Bristol service operated on weekdays.

Bob Thursby takes up the story of subsequent Aer Lingus arrivals at Rhoose:

It was at about midday each day that the Aer Lingus Dakota arrived at Rhoose. Many local kids from Rhoose village and Barry cycled to the airport to witness the spectacle. Nobody had thought of security in those days – you just turned up and watched. The imminent arrival of the aircraft was heralded by the appearance of the van from Pengam carrying the air traffic control staff, followed by a Western Welsh coach transporting the out-bound passengers. Navigation aids were minimal

Work underway at Rhoose in early 1954 – Aer Lingus worked around the contractors' construction work. The double Nashcrete building in the lower left became the core of Rhoose's 'new' terminal building. (Via N. Williams)

at the time and the terminal facilities were rudimentary. A nice touch once the Dakota had landed and was taxiing in was the appearance of a hand out of the side cockpit window and the Irish tri-colour on a short pole was inserted in to a holder above the flight deck roof.

BEA (British European Airways) were responsible for handling the daily Aer Lingus flight at Rhoose with Reg Bowers in charge, assisted by Harry Fox.

Summer 1952 Aer Lingus Schedule at Rhoose
Dublin to Rhoose

Flt No	Dep DUB	Arr CWL	10.06–02.07	03.07–17.07	18.07–30.09	01.10–25.10
EI300	08.55	10.30	Sat	Tue, Thu, Sat	Tue, Thu, Sat	Sat
EI302	15.10	16.45				Mon, Wed, Fri
EI302	16.15	17.50	Mon, Fri	Mon, Fri	Mon, Wed, Fri	

Rhoose to Dublin

Flt No	Dep CWL	Arr DUB	10.06–02.07	03.07–17.07	18.07–30.09	01.10–25.10
EI301	11.00	12.40	Sat	Tue, Thu, Sat	Tue, Thu, Sat	Sat
EI303	17.15	18.55				Mon, Wed, Fri
EI303	18.20	20.00	Mon, Fri	Mon, Fri	Mon, Wed, Fri	

Winter 1952; 1954 Schedule
Dublin to Rhoose (onwards to Bristol)

Flt No	Dep DUB	Arr CWL	Arr BRS
EI280	11.15	12.40	13.15

Bristol to Dublin (with stop at Rhoose)

Flt No	Dep BRS	Dep CWL	Arr DUB
EI281	14.05	14.40	16.10

For winter 1953/54, as for the previous winter, a stop at Rhoose was combined with the Dublin to Bristol service as winter demand would not sustain separate services to both these destinations. The flight numbers were the same as for winter 1952/53, outbound times from Dublin were the same, but the return times from Bristol and Rhoose were sixty-five minutes later. Full freight services were also operated by Aer Lingus on the Dublin–Rhoose–Bristol route.

Aer Lingus soldiered on at Rhoose almost unchallenged between 1952 and 1954, when their exclusivity at Rhoose was interrupted with the arrival of the 'outcasts' from Pengam, notably CAS (Cambrian Air Services), who had to move following the decision to close Pengam for commercial air services. The Welsh Advisory Council for Civil Aviation recommended that the Ministry of Transport and Civil Aviation (MTCA) take over Rhoose from the Air Ministry and the die was cast for the future of Rhoose as Cardiff's civil airport. MTCA spent £30,000 on strengthening and resurfacing the runway and some of the wartime buildings were converted for use as a terminal building. A T2 hangar located at Withybush Airport, north of Haverfordwest, was dismantled, transported to Rhoose and re-erected at a cost of £100,000. This hangar formed the basis of the Cambrian Airways maintenance facility, and survived until 2002, latterly as home for a fleet of privately owned light aircraft. Degradation of the hangar's structure and corrosion meant it was uneconomic to repair and one of Rhoose's landmarks for almost fifty years was condemned and demolished.

The first major 'rugby airlift' to use Rhoose was for the Ireland *v.* Wales international in March 1956 (see Chapter 7). Not only did Aer Lingus become the first scheduled civil airline user of Rhoose, it notched up many other firsts. The turboprop Fokker F.27 Friendship was introduced to service by Aer Lingus in December 1958. A series of demonstration flights was planned at the various airports that the airline was currently serving using its DC-3s. The airline was then the first to put the Fokker F.27 Friendship turboprop into passenger service and started scheduled operations with this type at Cardiff, replacing their trusty Douglas Dakotas. Their first F.27-100, EI-AKA (10105) *St Fintan* was delivered in November 1958. The whine of the Friendship's Dart turboprops became a familiar and welcome sound at Rhoose, the aircraft's first demonstration flight touching down on 9 December 1958 after a visit to Bristol. Two days later it was flown on demonstrations to Glasgow and Edinburgh and, on 15 December, to Paris. Aer Lingus still employed DC-3s to operate freighter services from Dublin to seven UK destinations including Rhoose.

At 1139hrs on 30 January 1959 another 'first' for Aer Lingus at Rhoose was the arrival of one of the airline's four-engine, turboprop Vickers V.808 Viscounts (EI-AJI) and in April Cambrian Airways took over from BEA as Aer Lingus' handling agent at Rhoose. The official opening of

One of Aer Lingus's first flights from Rhoose to Dublin in 1952 – the condition of the airfield was poor. (Robert C. Thursby)

Cork's new airport was on Monday 16 October 1961, with Aer Lingus operating several daily flights to London (Heathrow), three operating non-stop with Viscounts, plus two Friendships via Rhoose and two Friendships via Bristol. When the winter schedule came into force on 1 November there were two daily non-stop flights (except Sunday) between Cork and London and two via Rhoose and two via Bristol, all with Friendships. Cambrian Airways had also started serving Cork from Bristol, London and Rhoose with Dakotas, operating in association with Aer Lingus. From 1 June 1962, the Cork to London service was operated daily and non-stop with Friendships, but from 17 June onwards the larger Viscounts were used. A separate Cork–Rhoose–Bristol service was introduced from 1 June with Friendships, initially operated twice weekly, but increased to thrice weekly for the period from 23 July to 19 August

Fokker Friendships also operated a fortnightly Dublin to Jersey inclusive tour charter series for Universal Travel in the summer of 1963, and whilst the aircraft operated non-stop from Dublin to Jersey, a fuel stop was required at Rhoose on the return sector. Aer Lingus' last two Friendships continued in service until early June 1966, mostly operating on the Dublin to Bristol, Dublin to Rhoose, Dublin to Edinburgh and Dublin to Blackpool services, plus some weekend services to Glasgow and the Isle of Man. This twin turboprop that had revolutionised short-haul travel in the UK and many other parts of the world was then withdrawn from service by Aer Lingus and the airline's Viscounts took over the Dublin to Rhoose schedule and routes to the UK provincial destinations.

Aer Lingus Traffic Statistics (Passenger Numbers)

Year	Dublin–Rhoose	Cork–Rhoose
1955/56	8,668	
1956/57	6,996	
1957/58	12,340	
1958/59	7,787	
1959/60	13,572	
1960/61	14,151	
1961/62	14,013	220
1962/63	13,607	1,503
1963/64	16,234	1,746

The pending replacement by Aer Lingus of their 65-seat Viscount fleet with 113-seat Boeing 737 jets led to a reappraisal of the airline's more marginal routes, and the Cork–Rhoose–Bristol route was one of these. It had operated continuously since October 1961, but Aer Lingus noted that the service was giving poor financial returns despite heavy marketing support; the final factor in the demise of service on this route was the introduction of a new Swansea to Cork car ferry service in the summer of 1969, and the forthcoming withdrawal from service of the airline's Viscount fleet.

On 9 March 1970 Aer Lingus landed the first jet airliner at Cardiff on the newly completed 7,000ft runway 13/31, even though the plan was for it to be a Cambrian Airways BAC1-11. Aer Lingus Boeing 737-248 EI-ASG *Cormac* was that first jet airliner at Rhoose, followed ten minutes later by Cambrian's BAC1-11 with Captain Geoff Perrott at the controls – the aircraft had been stuck overnight at Bristol with airframe icing. On 12 March at 1644hrs one of Aer Lingus' new BAC1-11s EI-ANG operating the EIN6304/5 from and to Dublin on a rugby airlift charter landed at Rhoose – two further Aer Lingus BAC1-11s (EI-ANE and H) visited three days later, again on rugby charter flights. During a rugby airlift at 0958hrs on 3 March 1978 Aer Lingus operated the EIN3304 from Dublin, landing the first Boeing 747 to use the Welsh airport, EI-ASI, a 747-148 named *St Colmcille* (c/n 19744, Aer Lingus' first, delivered to them on 15 December 1970); it returned to Dublin as the EIN3305 at 1226hrs that day.

For summer 1970 Viscounts were scheduled on the Dublin to Rhoose, Dublin to Edinburgh, Dublin to Leeds/Bradford, Shannon to Belfast and Dublin to Cork routes. The BAC1-11s and

Aer Lingus Douglas Dakota freighter on the east end of the Cambrian-dominated south-side apron around 1958. (Gary Hilliard)

Aer Lingus continued to use their Douglas DC-3 fleet on freight flights to Rhoose long after passenger F27 services were introduced – this is EI-ACE in 1964. (Geoff Jones)

Aer Lingus V.808 Viscount EI-AJJ parked on the south-side apron in 1964. (Geoff Jones)

Rhoose in the 1950s – note the wartime dispersals alongside the northern (right) taxi-way and the white dots running across the airport from left to right marking the edges of the grass air strip. (Via Robert C. Thursby)

Rhoose's new control tower was complete in 1970, but the old south-side terminal and parking apron were still in use as Aer Lingus Boeing 737 EI-ASE taxies in. (Geoff Jones)

The first Boeing 747 'Jumbo Jet' to land at Rhoose, Aer Lingus's EI-ASI on 3 March 1978. (Eddie Maloney Collection)

EI-AVG at Rhoose in August 1988, one of three new Romanian-built BAC1-11's that joined the fledgling fleet of Ryanair in that year. (Geoff Jones)

Launch of Ryanair's three-times-weekly service from Dublin to Rhoose in 1978 – Ian Cran, airport director at the time, is on the left. (Cardiff Airport)

Boeing 737s were used on the remaining UK services, as well as on some flights on the Dublin to Rhoose and Dublin to Edinburgh routes. The last Aer Lingus Viscounts were withdrawn from service at the end of October 1970, so the airline's winter 1970/71 timetable featured an all-jet operation, with significant use of the Boeing 737 on routes from Dublin to UK destinations, including Rhoose. Many of these 737 operations were operated as 'combi' ones, mixed passenger and freight configurations, with two cargo pallets and seventy-four seats.

On the airline's UK provincial network, Boeing 737s were heavily deployed on most routes in summer 1971, with twelve of the thirteen weekly services on Dublin to Birmingham, all four Dublin to Bristol and all seven Dublin to Bristol and Rhoose, all fourteen Dublin to Glasgow and all seven Dublin to Leeds/Bradford services on the type. Again many of these were in combi configuration and feeding into Aer Lingus' transatlantic operation.

It was therefore a sad day when in March 1977 Aer Lingus operated its last scheduled flight to Rhoose; simultaneously they also dropped their Dublin to Leeds/Bradford route. The decision was part of a route rationalisation with British Airways, and whilst Aer Lingus had a monopoly on the daily Dublin to Bristol route, they were granted an increased share of the Dublin to Birmingham route. Part of the reason behind the rationalisation was a change in British Airways' operating pattern, which involved serving Dublin from Rhoose, Leeds/Bradford, Liverpool and Newcastle with one of BA's Rhoose-based Viscounts. The long-standing Dublin–Rhoose route reverted to Viscounts for a while. A young and upcoming independent carrier, Ryanair, was waiting in the wings and took over from the BA Viscounts in December 1987, initially flying thrice-weekly schedules with an Embraer EMB-110 Bandeirante (EI-BPI) and then the following year increasing to a daily schedule using Rombac BAC1-11 (EI-BSG, 'SS and 'VG), substituted later by Boeing 737-200s. When Ryanair flew its last service from Rhoose on 30 April 2006, Aer Arann immediately stepped in to take over the service.

However, the green shamrock of the Irish national carrier was to reappear at Rhoose in spring 2010. Since 2006 Irish regional Aer Arann had been flying several daily scheduled flights to Rhoose from Dublin and Cork using ATR-42 and ATR-72 turboprops – they stepped in to the void left when Air Wales ceased scheduled operations to operate the Cardiff–Cork route and then on 1 May 2006 took over from Ryanair on the twice-daily Cardiff–Dublin route. Ryanair announced at very short notice that it was ceasing operations at Cardiff International and transferring its flights from Dublin to Bristol due to 'extortionate increases in passenger charges'; managers at Cardiff disputed this claim and at the same time announced that Aer Arann was taking over the service five days later.

By 2008 Aer Arann, which had been founded in 1970 to service the three Aran islands off Ireland's west coast, had expanded and diversified with a fleet of eleven ATRs, and under the chairmanship of Padraig O'Ceidigh employed 380 staff operating schedules from Dublin, Cork, Galway and the Isle of Man. On 24 June 2008 Aer Arann signed an interline agreement with Aer Lingus and in January 2010 this took a further step forward when the two airlines agreed to jointly establish Aer Lingus Regional with the specific aim of developing 'hub' operations at both Dublin and Cork airports. This agreement resulted in the painting of the Aer Arann ATR fleet in the traditional green/white livery of Aer Lingus, with the aircraft bearing the name Aer Lingus Regional on the forward fuselage and small notification 'Operated by Aer Arann' alongside the passenger boarding door. The famous flying shamrock has thus returned to Rhoose fifty-eight years after its epoch-making first appearance. On 26 August 2010 Aer Arann was placed in the protection of the Irish High Court from its creditors, but continued to operate all services, including those to Rhoose. In the two years prior to this the airline is claimed to have lost €12 million and required financial rather than operational restructuring.

3

PENGAM MOORS CLOSES AND CAMBRIAN ARRIVES

Aer Lingus, plus handling agents BEA, had got things going operationally at Rhoose. The infrastructure needed a major overhaul and facilities needed to be improved. The 3,700ft runway 13/31 and 4,534ft runway 12/22, whilst adequate, were not over-generous for all-weather operations by increasingly sophisticated and larger aircraft, the Vickers Viscount and Douglas DC-4 in particular. However, they were hugely better than Pengam Moors and commercial night flying would be possible at Rhoose.

USAAF Douglas Dakotas had flown in and out of Pengam Moors during the war, but the field was too small for safe operations by the type. Airlines now had to comply with new and stricter civil legislation about commercial aircraft operations and the 'techniques' the Americans used at Pengam Moors did not comply with civil safety requirements.

On 1 April 1954 all commercial civil flying was transferred from Pengam Moors to Rhoose and this meant a mass migration for Cambrian Air Services (CAS), as it was then known. However, before this other commercial flights were starting to use Rhoose in addition to Aer Lingus. On Saturday 27 March an Air France flight arrived carrying supporters for that afternoon's rugby international at Cardiff Arms Park and on 2 April the *Western Mail* reported the arrival of a KLM flight. The 'new' and dismantled T2 hangar had already arrived from Withybush and had been erected on the south side of the airport, a terminal building was being established and administration buildings, both formed from the wartime Nashcrete buildings. Prior to the move to Rhoose, CAS's fleet comprised DH.89 Dragon Rapides, DH.104 Doves, Auster Autocrat G-AGYT and two Airspeed Consuls (these never entered service with CAS) – the opportunity to fly services from the all-weather hard runways at Rhoose meant that CAS's management quickly took the decision to augment the fleet with two larger Douglas Dakotas, G-AMSW and 'SX, both acquired from Air Service Training at Hamble in Hampshire. The arrival of Cambrian's Dakotas also meant the start of a new era for the airline and for Rhoose with the need to employ their first flight attendants. Pam Morris was the first, with Nora Nichols, Julie Downie, Dawn Sykes and Barbara Williams following soon after, part of a complement that soon grew to fourteen Rhoose-based girls to cover flights to Paris, the Channel Islands, Cork, Manchester and Glasgow.

Bob Thursby again casts his memory back to the very basic Rhoose in the mid-1950s:

> The original Port Road was retained to serve as the north entrance to the airfield (the fire station was located close to the point where it entered the airfield boundary). The 'new' military concrete road that was constructed towards Rhoose village mated up with Fontagary Road and formed the south-eastern boundary of the airfield. The present road from Rhoose village up to and somewhat

The Cambrian DH104 Dove G-AKSK on the east end of the apron at Rhoose sometime in 1954. (Ken Wakefield)

Cambrian's Dragon Rapide G-ALAT, named *Anglesey*, pictured in 1955 in front of the hangar at Rhoose, which was not exclusively used by Cambrian and also used to hangar light aircraft. (Ken Wakefield)

Cambrian Dragon Rapide G-ALZJ was acquired in 1950 whilst the airline was still based at Pengam Moors. It is seen here at Rhoose *c.*1955, named *Caernarvon*, and was maroon with a cream cheat line. (Mike Kemp)

beyond the current location of the fire station, is the last remaining part of it. When I first remember the airfield, the main entrance was off the concrete road some hundred yards or so on the Barry side of the present fire station. It boasted a 'gate guardian' in the form of a black painted, three-bladed propeller with MTCA painted on it in white [Ministry of Transport and Civil Aviation]. Immediately inside the main entrance on the right was a small Nashcrete building which must have been the wartime guardroom and which was later occupied by the MTCA police. There were no hangars, the main apron, somewhat smaller than it subsequently became, was where it was from pre-1954 up until 1971/72 when the new terminal was built. There were two concrete buildings, one of which many years later became the HQ of the Glamorgan and Pegasus Flying Clubs, and the other to the north of it, until the late 1960s, served as the staff canteen, also dispensing ice cream

Douglas Dakota G-AMSW, the first acquired by the airline, in its original CAS (Cambrian Air Services) colours on delivery to Rhoose in 1954. (Ken Wakefield)

Cambrian's first two Douglas Dakotas (G-AMSW and 'SX) arrived at Rhoose in 1954 and can be seen here in front of the Cambrian maintenance hangar. (Mike Kemp)

From top

The pristine Cambrian Airways check-in desk in the terminal at Rhoose in the 1950s, staffed by the delightful and ever-helpful Norma Nicholas and Pam Morris. (Ken Wakefield)

Cambrian Heron G-AOGU at Rhoose soon after delivery in 1956 – it was sold to Metropolitan in May 1959. (Geoff Jones)

The Cambrian duo G-AMSW Dakota and DH104 Dove G-AJOT on the Rhoose apron sometime around 1955 – the Dove was sold by Cambrian in November 1956. (Robert C. Thursby)

The terminal buildings at Rhoose in the early 1960s with a grass area fringing the edge of the apron and Cambrian aircraft steps very much in evidence. (Via Robert C. Thursby)

Cambrian's Capt. Geoff Perrott retired in 1975, after accumulating 11,500 flying hours with Cambrian at Rhoose – from left to right: the late Brian Ainsworth (Cabin Services Superintendent); Stewardess Margaret Bond; Geoff Perrott; Stewardess Margaret Miles; and Senior First Officer John Phillips. After his last landing at Rhoose with passengers he took off again with just the crew and did a low-level 'beat-up' along the line of the runway – he was, after all, Cambrian's Flight Operations Manager! (Ken Wakefield Collection)

The Keeble family in January 2011, a Rhoose institution for much of the airport's seventy-year history – from left to right: Paul Keeble, a watch controller at Rhoose from 1980–94 and 1997 to the present and part-time flying instructor since 1989; then his father George, an eighty-seven-year-old former Cambrian captain; and Paul's son Nicholas, who qualified with his PPL in 2009 and is now an instructor at Aeros. Sadly George passed away in September 2011. (Paul Keeble)

and the like through the window to spectators in the public enclosure that was formed somewhat later. There was still an air-raid shelter in front of the main apron and air traffic control were in a number of rather temporary looking buildings where the concrete over-flow apron – or 'play-pen', was built in the early 1960's (to the west of the old control tower). The grass area was, I seem to remember, still being farmed.

This corroborates the comments from visitors to the 1958 PFA Fly-In at Rhoose (see Chapter 10) that the grass areas between the hard runways and the temporary grass landing area established were all extremely rough.

One of the first CAS aircraft to arrive at Rhoose was the CAS Dragon Rapide G-AGZJ flown by Capt. Geoff Perrott, an aircraft he had flown first in 1946 when employed by British American Air Services. Capt. Perrott joined Cambrian in 1952 and was soon appointed chief pilot, a post he held until his retirement in 1975. His son Timothy became a first officer on Cambrian BAC1-11s much later. Another long-serving Cambrian pilot who arrived at Rhoose soon after was Capt. George Keeble – he had been based at CAS's outstation at Haverfordwest, but was welcomed into the fold at Rhoose, soon to be flying Dakotas. George's sons have all been involved with aviation and two of them at Rhoose, Paul still working in air traffic control since joining them there in 1979 plus being a PPL instructor at Rhoose for twenty-one years, most recently at Aeros where he taught his son Nicholas to fly in 2010. George Keeble flew with Cambrian until 1974, transferring into British Airways' BAC1-11 fleet based at Birmingham and retiring as BA's eighth most senior captain in 1981. He died in September 2011, aged eighty-seven. On 23 May 1955 CAS changed its name to Cambrian Airways with their new Heron G-AOGO being the first to sport the new titles. Another unofficial Cambrian aircraft at the time was the personal aircraft of S. Kenneth Davies, founder and former chairman of Cambrian up until 1949, the Miles Messenger G-AKKN. S. Kenneth Davies' first aircraft, a DH60 Gipsy Moth G-ABOA, had been the first aircraft acquired by Cambrian when the company was formed in April 1935.

In summer 1954 Ken Wakefield moved to Rhoose with Cambrian, an ex-RAF Volunteer Reserve pilot who had been flying as first officer in a Dakota between Germany and Johannesburg. He joined Cambrian, based initially at Bristol Whitchurch, but was soon transferred to join CAS's other Rhoose-based pilots Arthur Townsend, George Keeble, Phil Hendy, Geoff Perrott, 'Tommy' Thomas, 'Bob' Carson and Ronnie de Wilde – these were soon joined by John Gibson and Lionel 'Robby' Roberts. He was flying Doves, Rapides and the Auster Autocrat, until the Dakotas came along, and remembers that a captain's annual salary then was £1,035 plus an enhancement of 13s 6d per hour for flying the thirty-two-seat Dakota. In the busy summer he was regularly flying twelve two-hour duty days, six days a week, flying between six and eight sectors a day, and in the Doves and Rapides single-pilot. Heady stuff and hard work with no autopilots, but at least he was home every night. Winter 1954/55 was much quieter for Cambrian, with pilots enjoying two or three days off a week. Capt. Geoff Perrott and Ken Wakefield collected Cambrian's second Dakota (G-AMSX) from Hamble and flew it to Rhoose, via Bristol Whitchurch for a few 'touch and goes', on 24 November 1954. Conversion to a thirty-two-seat configuration followed at Rhoose ready for service entry in spring 1955 on Cambrian's Channel Islands services and replacement of the Dove on the Rhoose–Bristol–Southampton–Paris service.

New Cambrian routes from Rhoose to Belfast, Manchester and Nice in 1956 coincided with the arrival of the first of four DH.114 Heron (G-AOGO) four-engine aircraft that Cambrian had bought and which could carry between fourteen and seventeen passengers depending on loadings. The Auster was still being used as a company 'hack' and Doves, Rapides and, of course, Dakotas were still regularly flying passenger schedules from Rhoose with a batch of new pilots also arriving at Rhoose, including Terry Crook, Tony Stickland and Dick Twomey.

In May 1956 the *Barry & District News* reported that in March 1956 passenger numbers totalled 4,300 at Rhoose, 162 per cent higher than in March 1955, but by August were running a story about the apparent danger of low-flying aircraft to traffic on the concrete road between

Cambrian's four-engine DH.114 Heron G-AOGO, photographed shortly after delivery in 1956 over the Bristol Channel near Rhoose, and the first to wear the airline's new livery – this aircraft was sold in January 1959, but continued to frequent Rhoose in the colours of Morton Air Services. (Ken Wakefield)

Cambrian's former Chairman S. Kenneth Davies flew his own Miles M.38 Messenger G-AKKN from Rhoose during the 1950s, Welsh flag on the tail. (Robert C. Thursby)

Barry and Rhoose when aircraft were landing on Runway 31. They said that the authorities were considering the installation of warning lights on the road, to be controlled from the tower when aircraft were on finals to land. However, the mood at Rhoose was one of optimism as Cambrian's plans appeared positive and the passenger total carried for the financial year 1956/57 totalled 46,044, over a 30 per cent increase on the previous year.

However, on another front the whole future of Rhoose was being questioned in 1957 when speculation was rife that it had been proposed to transfer operations from Rhoose to RAF St Athan. A month later, in March, concern for Rhoose's future was again said to be in the balance following the decision to erect the new ITV television mast at St Hilary. Despite all these 'brick-bats' Rhoose's main operator, Cambrian, was gaining momentum and on 18 April 1957

Right One of Cambrian's Dakotas undergoing ground running, parked on the taxiway between the watch tower and the Cambrian hangar in the 1950s. (Garry Hilliard)

Below Aerial view of the south-east corner of Rhoose airport in the early 1960s. (Garry Hilliard)

Cambrian Viscount G-AMOP, in 1967, about to touch down on runway 31, the shorter runway at Rhoose, the captain obviously about to make use of every last foot of tarmac. A small BAS logo can just be seen on the forward cheatline. (Geoff Jones)

the airline inaugurated a scheduled service from Rhoose to Manchester using one of their four-engine DH Herons – this was part of a Manchester–Rhoose–Bristol–Jersey service. There was only one passenger on the first flight from Rhoose, a Mr Alf Dobson, the works manager for J. Collis & Son. This coincided with the closure of Bristol's former airport at Whitchurch and the official opening of the new airport at Lulsgate on 29 April. Cambrian Heron G-AORJ positioned in from Rhoose to operate the first commercial service at Lulsgate on 15 April flown by Capt. Denys Axel-Berg and First Officer Terry Crook, plus hostess Rosemary Jac. Capt. Axel-Berg was a distinctive, bearded and larger-than-life figure at the airport, and had already become affectionately known as the Colossus of Rhoose!

The dour speculation about Rhoose's future from 1957 was obviously buried, because in July 1958 it was reported that £30,000 had been spent on improvements to the airport in time for the British Empire and Commonwealth Games, which were held in Cardiff between 18 and 26 July. John Morgan also took over from John H. Watts as chairman of Cambrian in July. The year 1958 was proving to be a rollercoaster ride for Cambrian and Rhoose, with scheduled services flown to the Channel Islands, Southampton and Paris. On 7 February the state-owned British European Airways (BEA) acquired a 33 per cent interest in Cambrian, strengthening its role as a feeder airline and consolidating the importance of Rhoose Airport. However, the games in Cardiff may have had the opposite effect and, rather than stimulate traffic at Rhoose, it is thought that holidaymakers, also concerned about a worldwide economic recession and credit crunch, stayed at home. Cambrian's financial situation was precarious with closure of the airline contemplated, forcing the termination of its winter 1958/59 programme and the sale of all its aircraft except one Dragon Rapide (G-AJCL). An operating loss of £53,473 was reported for the year ending 31 December 1958, increased to £102,380, with the capital loss on disposal of the fleet and BEA's investment in Cambrian written down. The Manchester–Jersey schedule via Rhoose and Bristol was maintained, although flown by a Jersey Airlines Heron.

The 1958 traffic statistics for Rhoose, with Cambrian responsible for most, were a total of 18,018 movements, 5,196 of them by commercial air transport aircraft. Passenger numbers totalled 46,357, a quarter of which (11,178) were transit passengers. Air freight totalled 222.1 tons. This placed Rhoose as the seventeenth-busiest UK airport in terms of passengers handled, although some of those airports that were busier are not now significant commercial air transport airports, including, Lydd and Lympne in Kent. Rhoose's long-time rival airport, Bristol, reported 39,573 passengers in 1958, yet Stansted was a mere backwater then with only 20,003 passengers.

Cambrian was relaunched in 1959 with John Morgan, the well-known head of one of Wales' leading civil engineering contractors (his company built the Heads of the Valleys Road), appointed the new chairman – Wing Commander 'Bill' Elwin joined him as managing director. Cambrian leased three DC-3 'Pionairs' (modified Dakotas) from BEA, with G-AHCZ, G-AGIP and G-ALXL arriving at Rhoose where services were successfully relaunched on 2 March 1959. These were Liverpool to Jersey via Rhoose and Bristol and Rhoose to Paris via Bristol and Southampton. Rhoose was now very much back in business, the Rhoose to Manchester service (via Bristol) relaunched later in 1959 and the three DC-3s were purchased from BEA, plus two more DC-3s (G-AMFV and 'JX). BEA, who had been Aer Lingus' handling agent at Rhoose since 1952, pulled out of the airport altogether and in April 1959 Cambrian took over as their handling agent. Cambrian posted a £40,025 profit for 1959 and the airline was on the road to success.

Early in the 1960s both Fokker and Handley Page tried to sell their twin-engine turbo-props to Cambrian as a DC-3 replacement, the F.27 Friendship and Dart Herald respectively. The HPR.7 Dart Herald demonstrator G-APWA visited Rhoose from the company base at Radlett in Hertfordshire on 5 April 1961, flown by Squadron Leader H.G. Hazleden, and flew two demo flights that day before its return to Radlett. Cambrian placed an initial order for one of the type, and was allegedly considering an order for four. In April 1962 BEA transferred its Irish Sea routes to Cambrian, plus the services from the Isle of Man with the Liverpool to Belfast route and the order for the Herald was cancelled. BEA had been losing £500,000 a year on these routes, so the deal was for Cambrian to buy five of BEA's older and smaller Viscount 701s, operate the new routes and take over the ground handling at Liverpool. The arrival of the first Cambrian Viscount G-AMOPs at Rhoose was disrupted by the severe snowy weather of

Taxiing past the familiar control/watch tower in 1962, Cambrian Dakota G-AGHM had been acquired from BEA the previous year. (Peter Phillips)

1963, but at 1600hrs on 6 January 'OP arrived from Heathrow – in the following days extensive crew training with the Viscount was carried out throughout the Cambrian network. On 28 January 1963 the second Viscount G-AMOG arrived at Rhoose flown by Capt. George Keeble in the striking new livery ready for the airline's – and Rhoose's – first commercial Cambrian Viscount service, a Welsh rugby supporters flight to Edinburgh on 30 January. In the same month work began on a £70,000 extension to the Cambrian maintenance hangar in order to accommodate the Viscounts and to complement the company's infamous 'White House' administrative building which had been opened a few months earlier. The first scheduled Cambrian Viscount (G-AMOP) service was on 20 February to Bristol and Cork and then from Cork to Heathrow. The former BEA Irish Sea routes were fully inaugurated by Cambrian on 1 April, the fleet of Viscounts now numbering four. Cambrian's network-wide passenger figures for 1962 shot up to 115,000, and more than doubled to 256,000 in 1963 thanks to the inauguration of the Viscount schedules.

The Viscounts enabled Cambrian to open up many new routes from Rhoose – and other UK airports including Exeter and Southampton – the most significant being the 1964 programme from Rhoose and Bristol to Palma, Majorca, followed by Rimini, Barcelona, Ostend, Valencia and Zagreb. The mid-1960s was the heyday for the Cambrian Viscount fleet at Rhoose and by 1967 they were operating a fleet of eleven of the type, and the list of destinations had grown still further, supported by sister company Cambrian Holidays.

Cambrian was recruiting pilots in the 1960s, one of whom was Bob Thursby who had learnt to fly at Glamorgan Flying Club in 1959/60. Bob, along with other 'cadets', was sent to Perth in Scotland in 1965 for training, and actually joined Cambrian in 1967 when their fleet comprised five Dakotas and eleven ex-BEA Viscounts.

During the early 1960s Cambrian had a contract with Gibraltar-based airline Gibair to service their sole aircraft, the Dakota G-AMFV which they had bought from Cambrian at the end of 1962 and which was delivered the following March. This was then seen annually in the Cambrian maintenance hangar, and in autumn 1966 Cambrian leased their G-AGHS to Gibair for a short while when 'FV was unserviceable. It was at this time that late one evening at Rhoose some anonymous joker painted the letters 'YO' in front of the Gibair name on the nose of the aircraft. Two other of Cambrian's now familiar DC-3s were also retired at the same

Former Cambrian Dakota G-AGHM is still around in 2011, preserved as a work of art on a roundabout in Jeddah, Saudi Arabia. (Susie Johnson-Khalil)

Viscount G-AMON
in BAS/Cambrian
colours in the early
1970s. (Peter Metherell
Collection)

time, G-AGIP and G-AMJX, and they remained at Rhoose behind the maintenance hangar until in August 1963, when they were purchased by the King of Morocco (CN-ALI and 'LJ respectively) and flown from Rhoose to Prestwick for overhaul by Scottish Aviation.

Cambrian's five Dakotas, more correctly Pionairs, had an enviable service record. All five were used in February 1965 to ferry rugby supporters from Rhoose to Edinburgh and back, making two round trips each, some returning to Swansea, and were complemented by British Midland Argonauts and Dakotas. During 1968 Cambrian decided to withdraw the Pionair fleet from service. The Bristol–Rhoose–Dinard service was flown for the last time on 4 September by G-ALXL; one passenger I talked to who had used this Dinard service remembers the lack of a PA (passenger announcement) that modern airline passengers are familiar with. Instead the Cambrian captain, at an appropriate moment mid-flight, would write the relevant details on a piece of paper, the cruising altitude, the speed, the estimated time of arrival, the weather at the destination, etc. and pass this paper back down the cabin for the passengers to read. The Pionairs also flew their last services to Belfast, Jersey, Manchester and Glasgow during the autumn of 1968 and the final day of Cambrian scheduled Pionair services from Rhoose was on 31 October, when Capt. Ronnie de Wilde flew G-AHCZ from Rhoose via Bristol to Southampton and Paris (Le Bourget) and back. It was also the day that Captain de Wilde retired almost exactly ten years after he had arrived at Rhoose to join Cambrian.

Four of the Pionairs were sold to World Inter Sales Services Ltd and on various dates in 1969 and 1970 were ferried from Rhoose via Nice to their temporary home in Cyprus, the Cambrian titles painted out and Cypriot registrations 5B-CBA, 'B, 'C and 'D substituted (they were G-AGHS, G-ALXL, G-AHCZ and G-AGHM respectively). 'HS and 'CZ ended up in Beirut, Lebanon, 'XL in Bahrain and 'HM in Jeddah, Saudi Arabia. The first three were soon derelict and scrapped, but 'HM lives on, restored by the national airline Saudia, mounted on a pole above synthetic clouds and is located in the middle of a roundabout in Jeddah.

The year 1968 was also when Rhoose saw Cambrian's smart new livery for the first time, an updated and jet-styled Cambrian dragon in line with the airline's impending entry to the jet age. The company's name also appeared in a new lettering style, with the 'British Air Services' name appearing for the first time on its aircraft, and the fin was painted a darker blue, also bearing the Cambrian name and logo.

4

CAMBRIAN, BRITISH AIR SERVICES, BRITISH AIRWAYS

Cambrian Airways' early history at Rhoose has been covered in Chapter 3 – it has also been extensively documented in many publications and is celebrated on Garry Hillard's Cambrian web site (www.cambrianairways.org.uk), the 'original' site, opened in June 2003.

By 1966 Cambrian had a fleet of eight Viscounts and five Pionairs (converted Douglas Dakotas) and in the first six months broke all records, carrying 350,000 passengers system-wide, a 35 per cent increase from the first six months of 1965. But in 1967 John Morgan, Cambrian's chairman, announced an expected loss for the year estimated at £60,000 and that 1966's profit only represented an unsatisfactory 2 per cent of turnover. Cambrian needed more capital, so turned to BEA for help – Cambrian's problem mirrored another UK independent airline, Newcastle-based BKS (soon to be renamed Northeast Airlines) in which BEA had taken a 30 per cent stake in 1964. BEA wanted to keep both these airlines alive, but without having to operate them. They formed a holding company, British Air Services (BAS), 70 per cent owned by BEA, and BAS then acquired 100 per cent interest in both Cambrian and Northeast. The main benefit at Rhoose was that all Northeast aircraft maintenance (they had a fleet of Viscounts) was to be concentrated at Rhoose. The real situation though was that Cambrian had lost its independence, and though it gained some measure of financial security, it was on the slippery slope to oblivion.

The November 1968 collapse of British Eagle also benefitted Cambrian, who had been carrying 40 per cent of the traffic from Liverpool in competition with British Eagle. This suddenly shot up to 75 per cent and with 130 staff based at Liverpool the almost unthinkable idea of moving Cambrian's headquarters from Rhoose to Liverpool was proposed, but soon quashed. It was a bad time for UK independent airlines, and, as well as British Eagle, Transglobe, BUA (CI) and Air Ferry all ceased operations about this time.

Early in 1971 Cambrian began to withdraw their Viscount 701s from service, G-AMOA having been taken out of service as early as January 1970. The larger ex-BEA and British Airways Viscount 806s were replacing the 701s and by the end of 1971 Cambrian schedules from Rhoose and elsewhere were being flown by a mix of Viscounts and BAC1-11s. The oldest of the Cambrian Viscount fleet, G-ALWF (Const. No.5) and affectionately known by some Cambrian pilots as 'woolly fox', was acquired in February 1966 and flew its last revenue service on 24 December 1971. Its actual last flight was on 12 April 1972 when it flew from Rhoose to Heathrow then on to Liverpool. Now considered an historic aircraft as the oldest surviving Viscount airliner in the world, it is preserved at the Imperial War Museum collection at Duxford in Cambridgeshire, resplendent in its original 1950s BEA colours. However, the

Cambrian's 700 series Viscounts 'out to grass' at the rear of their maintenance hangar after their withdrawal from service. (Geoff Jones)

G-AOYN in British Airways colours, but with a small 'Cambrian' on the forward fuselage, on the main apron, ready to operate a schedule service in June 1975. (Geoff Jones)

The very last Viscount G-APIM leaves Rhoose after being serviced in December 1981. (Geoff Jones)

Cambrian BAC1-11 G-AVGP taxiing in from runway 13 in 1971. (Geoff Jones)

Left In 1966 Cambrian Airways chartered the Aer Turas Douglas DC-4 EI-AOR after one of its Viscounts had crashed. (Geoff Jones)

Below Cambrian chartered this Bristol Freighter G-APAV on several occasions in the early 1970s to repatriate Rolls-Royce Spey engines from their BAC1-11s to Rhoose for maintenance. (Kelvin Lumb)

Cambrian Viscount acquisition era was not over yet, and in 1969 British Airways Cambrian acquired G-ANRS, a former British Eagle Viscount 732, to use as a cabin services training unit – it was repainted in British Airways colours, the wings detached and placed on a plinth in front of the old terminal building on the airport's south side. It was given the spoof civil registration G-WHIZ and later ended up as part of the Wales Air Museum collection (see Chapter 12).

There are many apocryphal stories surrounding Cambrian and the whole commercial flying scene at Rhoose in this era, far less restrictive than today, an almost family atmosphere. Vince Cockett, an air traffic controller at Rhoose between 1966 and 1972 remembers several Viscount-related incidents, one when Capt. John Reid taxied to the threshold of runway 13 with a load of Paris-bound passengers when the RVR (runway visual range) was marginal. He waited on the threshold until the RVR improved slightly and took off, only to have an engine fire. Despite the poor visibility, air traffic control managed to talk the Viscount through a 180-degree turn, back on to the ground, this time landing on the reciprocal runway 31, the engine fire contained, but everyone thankful that despite the poor visibility they were able to land. Transferred to a replacement Viscount they tried again – this time the undercarriage wouldn't retract after take-off so once again the aircraft had to land back at Rhoose. The passengers and crew had had enough by then and were re-booked on subsequent flights.

The years 1970 and 1971 saw Cambrian's acquisition of former BEA Viscount 800 series aircraft, eight aircraft in all, the first G-AOYI in July 1970 and the last G-AOYN in December 1971. These were to continue to fly the Cambrian/BA schedules from Rhoose up until 1981, and in December that year the very last Viscount serviced at Rhoose, G-APIM, took off from the airport having been bought, like many of its sister aircraft in the fleet, by BAF (British Air Ferries).

The announcement that Cambrian was to acquire BAC1-11 jets in 1969, and the acquisition of the first one from Autair and Court Line via BAC, was an inevitable consequence of the ageing of the Viscount fleet and the forthcoming opening of the extended runway 13/31 at Rhoose that would allow the safe operation of the type from its home airport. When the new runway extension to 7,000ft was completed early in 1970, it wouldn't be long before Cambrian's first jet landed, although pipped at the post by ten minutes by an Aer Lingus jet (see Chapter 3) on 9 March 1970. This Cambrian BAC1-11 was flown by Capt. Geoff Perrott, who was undergoing line training under the supervision of Capt. Ken Wakefield in the right-hand seat. Prior to this, following Cambrian's intention to acquire BAC1-11 jets, both Ken Wakefield and George Keeble had spent the best part of a year flying BAC1-11s with Autair International to gain the necessary experience to qualify as training captains on the type. At the time of this 'first', Cambrian was busy training thirty pilots for their new BAC1-11 fleet.

Following the December 1969 delivery of Cambrian's first eighty-seat BAC1-11 jet, there were logistical issues that had to be solved – they weren't used on schedules until 1 April 1970. One ex-Cambrian pilot said in a rather exaggerated way, 'their engines were blowing up all over the place'. They may not have literally 'blown up' but undoubtedly 'went tech' on quite a few occasions. Repatriating the engines to Rhoose and vice versa became the job of Midland Air Cargo (MAC) and their Coventry-based fleet of four Bristol Super-Freighters that had been purchased from British Air Ferries at Lydd in Kent. MAC's first aircraft was G-APAV which arrived at Coventry in October 1970 – G-AMLP, G-APAU and G-ANVR followed, although 'AU and 'AV handled most of their business between May 1971 and February 1973, when the airline folded. Cambrian Airways regularly chartered these two Super-Freighters and on the evening of 18 August 1971 G-APAV flew a 'sick' engine back home from Ibiza. The aircraft arrived from Coventry on 16 August at 2047hrs and left for Ibiza at 2302hrs. Midland Air Cargo was also chartered by the Ford Motor Co. to transport car parts to Germany and in September 1971 the same aircraft flew a charter from Rhoose to Saarbrücken and from Hanover to Rhoose. Problems with the BAC1-11 in August 1970 also resulted in Cambrian having to charter a Braathens SAFE Douglas DC-6B, one of nine examples in this Norwegian charter company's fleet. On 1 August the 1608hrs arrival at Rhoose of this replacement aircraft from Oslo, LN-SUB, was a rare treat for enthusiasts and spectators, now getting used to turboprops and jets, but for the Cambrian passengers whose flight was nearly eight hours late a welcome relief to at last be on their way to Palma at 1702hrs. The aircraft returned from Palma to Rhoose the following day before positioning to London Heathrow empty and was back the following weekend doing exactly the same.

Cambrian's last Dakota service between Paris and Rhoose was flown on 31 October 1968 by G-AHCZ under the command of Capt. Ronnie de Wilde. The airline's Dakota/Pionair fleet had operated from Rhoose for fourteen years and system-wide had flown 8 million miles, carrying over 1 million passengers. Not bad for an aircraft with only thirty-two passenger seats.

Rhoose saw its fair share of Cambrian BAC1-11s, many of them at the weekends when released from scheduled responsibilities flying for BEA in Germany and for BEA between Liverpool and Heathrow, Birmingham and Dublin and Manchester and Dublin. By 1971 Cambrian had acquired its fourth BAC1-11. They frequently flew for Cambrian Air Holidays in competition with the increasing dominance of the Clarkson/Hourmont Travel Group, who were using Court Line and Britannia aircraft to fly their passengers.

Cambrian's maintenance ramp at the rear of their hangar hosted two unexpected visitors during 1975 when British Airways Scottish, basically the subsidiary airline operating the airline's highlands and islands routes, flew its two Short SC.7 Skyliners (G-AZYW and G-BAIT), a nineteen-passenger version of the utility Skyvan aircraft, to Rhoose prior to their sale to Busy Bee Air Services in Norway. These Glasgow-based aircraft had replaced DH.114 Herons on these public service obligation Scottish services in March/April 1973.

The morphing of Cambrian Airways through British Air Services (along with Northeast) into British Airways Regional Division (BA RD) occurred in the early 1970s, a grouping that also included BEA Scottish Airways and the Channel Islands Division. The equipment of choice was the venerable Vickers Viscount, although the 700 series Viscounts that had propelled Cambrian and Rhoose into the turboprop age had been superseded by the larger V.800 Viscounts, many ex-British European Airways (BEA) aircraft. On 1 September 1972 Cambrian Airways became an integral part of BA RD. One brief bout of rare BEA activity occurred in 1973 when BEA Tridents and BAC1-11s flew a series of weekly charters from Rhoose to Palma and other Spanish holiday destinations.

By 1977 British Airways was the main scheduled service operator at Rhoose, the services linking via Bristol to Paris, Dublin, Belfast and the Channel Islands. BA also acted as handling agents at Rhoose for some of the other scheduled operators and many of the charter flights. They were carrying in excess of 60,000 passengers a year from Rhoose on 1,100 separate services and using both Viscounts and BAC1-11 jets. Their station superintendent at the time was Fred Baker who had a team of four duty officers and five ground operations assistants.

With a new 7,000ft runway and new terminal to match, it was only a matter of time before Rhoose welcomed more 'wide-body' airliners. This term is a generality that has been used to describe the Boeing 747, the Douglas DC-10 and the Lockheed Tristar, all of which flew for the first time in the 1960s or 1970s, designed to carry 250+ passengers. The first wide-body to land at Rhoose was an Aer Lingus' Boeing 747 in March 1978 (see Chapter 2), but on 16 February 1979 British Airways G-BBAG became the first Lockheed L-1011-385-1 Tristar to land at Rhoose for a passenger flight, chartered to take the Welsh rugby team, officials and supporters from Cardiff to Paris. However, prior to this another BA Tristar had landed at Rhoose, a weather diversion from London Heathrow, but without passengers. Although the Tristar normally seated 330 passengers (thirty first class and 300 economy), on the 16 February flight the seating was changed to all economy, with 350 passengers accommodated. Ken Wakefield, who by now was flying the Tristar for British Airways from Heathrow, remembers the day: 'We positioned the aircraft from London Heathrow to Rhoose but were delayed in leaving Heathrow because the reconfiguration of the seating wasn't completed on time. Then when we arrived at Rhoose there was a further delay whilst the ground handlers found a suitable pair of access steps.' The occasion was a good photo opportunity and BA manager (Wales and South-West

Chartered by Cambrian in 1970 when one of its BAC1-11's 'went tech' in Palma, Majorca, this Norwegian-registered Braathens Douglas DC-6B LN-SUB carried the passengers south from Rhoose. (Kelvin Lumb)

Two of British Airways Scottish Division's Short Skyliners were stored at Rhoose in 1975, prior to their sale to Busy Bee Air Services in Norway. (Geoff Jones)

In British Airways colours, Viscount G-AOYG stands in the former Cambrian maintenance hangar in December 1981. (Mike Kemp)

Viscount G-AMON, now in British Airways colours. (Peter Metherell Collection)

Above In 1973–74 Cambrian chartered a BAC1-11, including crews, to Gulf Air – this may have influenced that airline's decision to acquire the ex-BA G-AXMU, seen here at Rhoose as A40-BU being prepared for delivery in November 1977. (Geoff Jones)

Right BA's Bryan Savage shakes the hand of Capt. Ken Wakefield after he landed British Airways Lockheed L1011 Tristar at Rhoose in February 1979, prior to operating a rugby charter to Paris. (Ken Wakefield Collection)

Below Cambrian employees at Rhoose outside the west end of the maintenance hangar with BAC1-11 G-BBMG. Cyril Tomlinson is second from the right in dungarees, one of the many staff still employed here. (Morley Williams)

MANAGER Wales and South West England Bryn Savage was on hand to congratulate Captain Ken Wakefield when he flew the first commercially-operated Tri-Star from Cardiff Airport.

It was a notable occasion, for the TriStar was on charter to fly the Welsh Rugby team, officials and supporters – a total of 330 – to Paris.

Captain Wakefield seems to make a habit of "firsts" – he flew the first-ever aircraft – a De Havilland Rapide into Cardiff Airport when it opened in 1954 and also the first British Airways jet on the opening of the new runway in 1969.

He and Mr Savage are old friends, for previously both were with Cambrian Airways. With them in the picture is Cardiff Station Manager Fred Baker.

BAF acquired many of the ex-Cambrian/BA Viscounts – G-AOYJ is being prepared at Rhoose, when BAF took over the former Cambrian maintenance hangar, for sale to Air Algerie in February 1982. (Geoff Jones)

De-icing two of Manx's Jetstream 31s one winter morning in December 1992. (Geoff Jones)

Parting out of former BA 747 G-BDXC at Rhoose in July 2002. (Malcolm Bradbury)

England) Bryn Savage was on hand, as well as BA's station manager at Rhoose, Fred Baker. Both Bryn Savage and Ken Wakefield were ex-Cambrian.

British Airways withdrew from scheduled operations at Rhoose on 31 March 1980, the end of an era that stretched back to CAS's arrival twenty-six years earlier. However, as one door closes, another opens, and Dan-Air stepped in to operate all of those scheduled routes previously operated by BA.

British Airways placed an order for twenty-one of the larger Boeing 747-400s in July 1990, all given names of UK cities. G-BNLC was flown to Rhoose on 23 October 1990 for the official naming ceremony, *City of Cardiff/Dinas Caerdydd*. This was a big day at Rhoose as it followed the announcement of a £70 million investment by BA at Rhoose in BAMC and the prospect of creating 1,200 jobs. A hand-picked, all-Welsh crew flew 747-400 G-BNLC to Rhoose for a naming ceremony and unveiling by Lord Mayor John Smith, accompanied by BA chairman Lord King. The band of the Royal Regiment of Wales and 100 members of *Cor Meibion De Cymru* gave the airliner a real Welsh welcome. Lord King said, 'It was a pleasure to visit Cardiff-Wales Airport for a second time in recent weeks [the first had been to announce the BAMC project] and reinforce our links with the city [of Cardiff] and its people'. In reply the airport chairman Ken Hutchings commented, 'We applaud BA's efforts to take the word *Caerdydd* around the world'.

British Airways schedules returned to Rhoose in 1995 when Manx Airlines became a BA franchisee (see Chapter 5), and since 1993 the omnipresent BAMC engineering base and a continual flow of BA Boeing 747, 767 and 777 airliners for maintenance sustain the airline's strong links with the airport. The demise of some of BA's older B747s has also occurred at Rhoose. G-AWNB flew its last commercial service from New York/JFK on 31 August 1998 before being ferried empty to Rhoose for decommissioning by BAMC and then departing for desert storage at Roswell, New Mexico. Sister ship 'NA, BA's first 747, surprised everyone at Rhoose (and Heathrow) when it arrived in November 1998 wearing full BOAC colours, before flying to Bruntingthorpe near Leicester for scrapping. BA's B747-200 fleet passed through Rhoose for decommissioning – one aircraft, G-BDXC, was towed to the end of the old runway 12 for parting out or scrapping in July 2002. Some of its sister ships were stored at Rhoose and four (G-BDXF, 'G, 'H and 'N) were delivered to Bournemouth-based European Air Charter. One of the others went to Air Atlanta Icelandic.

British Airways charters and training flights have also used Rhoose more recently. The airline's new Paris Orly-based, luxury-class start-up Open Skies, which followed the takeover of French airline L'Avion in August 2008, saw some of their Boeing 757-200 aircraft crew training at Rhoose, when prior to operating their first service in August 2009, they were flying multiple-sector crew experience flights. The September 2010 Ryder Cup and the BA B777 charter is covered in Chapter 7. An Open Skies Boeing 757 (the EC24) diverted to Rhoose on 24 October 2010 inbound from Newark to Paris Orly.

5

OTHER BASED AIRLINES

Wales's poor north–south road and rail infrastructure has tempted a stream of airline operators to try to operate a commercial air service between Rhoose and various destinations in North Wales. It was one of the many aims of the first Welsh Assembly government after May 1999 to establish a north–south PSO (public service obligation) air service.

Cambrian Air Services were involved in the first Welsh internal scheduled service, inaugurated on 11 April 1949, but from Pengam Moors and flown by BEA to Valley (Anglesey) via Liverpool and Chester (Hawarden) with Dragon Rapides. Cambrian were the booking and handling agents for BEA. Also in 1949 Cambrian had ambitiously filed a whole raft of route authority applications with the Air Transport Advisory Board, one of which was to operate schedules from Cardiff (Pengam Moors) to Liverpool, which was unsuccessful. CAS started schedules from Cardiff (Pengam Moors) to Liverpool in their own right on 9 April 1951 using a Dragon Rapide.

Most famously one of the first serious attempts at a north–south service was also one of Europe's first scheduled helicopter services. It was the state-owned airline BEA that inaugurated this trial service on 1 June 1950 using a Sikorsky S.51, flying from Liverpool Airport to Cardiff (Pengam Moors) with three passengers. But as this wasn't at Rhoose this merely puts future operations in context – the helicopter service ended on 31 March 1951. However, it did also mark the end of BEA flying from Cardiff, except for the airline's small passenger-handling unit established in 1952 for the first Aer Lingus flights to Rhoose (see Chapter 2). Pengam's closure and Cambrian's move to Rhoose also saw fleet changes with the five Dragon Rapides sold and two Douglas Dakotas acquired from air-service training at Hamble. These plied CAS's scheduled routes which included the north–south Liverpool to Rhoose at a single fare of £3 10s.

Dan-Air tried a new schedule in 1965 with one of its Douglas Dakotas, Teesside–Chester–Rhoose. They quickly realised the service wouldn't be a success, and after only twenty-seven days of operation on the route it was suspended from their schedule.

Air Wales, in its first manifestation, started operations at Rhoose with a Piper PA-31 Navajo Chieftain (G-BWAL) in December 1977. With Capt. John Evans as its Director of Operations, the airline's very first service was a south–north from Rhoose to Chester (Hawarden), a forty-minute 'hop' for the nine-seater aircraft. Air Wales flew the schedule twice a day and after two months reported 40 per cent load factors and 100 passengers a week using the service. Air Wales also froze its fares during the first twelve months of operation at £16.50 single in order to compete with fares on British Rail. The airline received a £10,000 grant from Clwyd County Council to help with start-up costs on the service.

Air Wales' first
aircraft, the Piper
Navajo Chieftain
G-BWAL, seen in
1977 at Rhoose with
passengers boarding
for the flight to Brest
and Cherbourg in
France. (Geoff Jones)

Highland Airways
Jetstream 31 G-EIGG,
one of those based at
Rhoose to operate
the PSO service
to Anglesey until
Highland went in to
receivership in 2010.
(Geoff Jones)

Manx2.com took
over the PSO service
from Highland in
2010 using one of
its Dornier Do228s
(D-CMNX) operated
for Manx2 by FLM
Aviation. (Geoff
Jones)

With the demise of Air Wales, another Rhoose-based company, RB Aviation Ltd, had aspirations to step in to the breach with a north–south scheduled air link (see Chapter 9). Using their nine-seat Piper PA-31 Navajo Chieftain, trading as Cambrian Air, they proposed to operate two flights on four days a week from Rhoose to Chester (Hawarden) and back – a proposal to extend the service to West Wales (Haverfordwest, Withybush) was also mooted. Services were flown with the Navajo, but often load factors were so low that the company's Aztec or Seneca were substituted, each able to carry five passengers. RB Aviation also offered air taxi services and were the owners of the Cambrian Flying Club at Rhoose. However, the north–south Welsh air link was soon dropped as uneconomic.

In May 1981 Euroair, based at Biggin Hill, inaugurated passenger services on the Rhoose to Chester route with a £37.50 single fare and flying a twin-engine Cessna Titan – this complemented the airline's Datapost night-time contract with Royal Mail to fly nightly from Rhoose to the Royal Mail's Liverpool air freight hub. Don Daines, Euroair's managing director, and Kim Vivian, commercial manager, were convinced the service 'would grow – we will then be able to consider a round-Wales airlink'. The first flight was flown by former Air Wales Captain Bryan Evans. In October 1981 an air charter and taxi company, Kraken Air, was formed to fly services from Rhoose and Swansea. When, in early 1982, Euroair's attempts at operating the schedule between Rhoose and Chester (Hawarden) failed, Kraken Air stepped in to the breach using their Piper PA-23 Aztec G-HARV and flew their first south–north service on 1 March. Another aspirant to the south–north schedule around 1982/83 was Manchester-based Telair, who commenced scheduled services out of Liverpool on the Liverpool–Chester (Hawarden)–Rhoose route on 1 March 1983 using one aircraft from their fleet of two BN-2 Islander aircraft (G-AXXH and 'WH). They also increased their utilisation by flying nightly Datapost services to Liverpool, until they ceased operations (see Chapter 6).

Following the Government of Wales Act 2006 the Welsh Assembly Government was established in 2007 and one of their first commitments was to recommence a Welsh north–south air link. This was inaugurated on 8 May 2007 by Highland Airways, an Inverness-based airline that since its formation in 1991 had specialised in Scottish scheduled services, distribution of newspapers to the northern and western isles of Scotland, plus Royal Mail flights to the Western Isles. Using one eighteen-passenger Jetstream 31 from their fleet of nine of the type, Highland based the aircraft at Rhoose to fly a twice daily rotation from Rhoose to Anglesey Airport – Maes Awyr Môn (RAF Valley). A £2.4 million subsidy was agreed for the route by the Assembly – in the first year of operations Highland carried 14,000 passengers on the route, many of them Assembly and government officials. Highland Airways ceased operations in March 2010 and went into administration, having flown 40,000 passengers on the route, but leaving passengers on this increasingly important and strategic route grounded. Fortunately Noel Hayes' Manx2 airline stepped in, and by Monday 10 May 2010 the twice-daily weekday schedule was reinstated, this time using a Manx2 nineteen-seat Dornier 228 (D-CMNX). In May Manx2 carried 480 passengers on the route and 828 in June – a re-tender process was then initiated by the Assembly for an operator for the next four years, commencing on 1 January 2011. The service had been nicknamed *Ieuan Air* after the Assembly's Deputy First Minister and Transport Minister Ieuan Wyn Jones who supported the service, but is heavily criticised by Welsh Liberal Democrats because of the magnitude of the financial subsidy provided. On 3 December 2010 Ieuan Wyn Jones announced that Manx2, with its partner FLM Aviation, had been successful in securing the Rhoose–Anglesey contract, with the annual government subsidy rising from £800,000 to £1.2 million. During August 2010 Manx2 provided onward connections from Anglesey to their Isle of Man base.

Air Wales No. 1

This Rhoose-based airline was founded in August 1977 with DK Aviation (aircraft brokers from Grimsby under the chairmanship of David King) and Orbit Trust as the main shareholders. Under the airline's slogan, 'The Dragon is Back on the Tail', the airline's first scheduled service was flown from Rhoose to Chester (Hawarden) on 6 December that year using their Piper PA-31 Navajo Chieftain G-BWAL. The chief pilot was Capt. John Evans, who was famed for his connections with the start-up of Brymon Airways. Air Wales added services from Rhoose to Cherbourg and Brest in France that winter and received an unexpected boost to passenger numbers in March 1978 when the oil tanker *Amoco Cadiz* ran aground on the 16th off the Brittany coast near Brest, boosting passenger requirements to reach the western tip of the Brittany peninsula.

Air Wales Timetable, Winter 1977/78

Flt No.	Day	Dept.	Arr.	Fare
Rhoose–Hawarden (Chester)				
XE403	MTWTF	0800	0840	£16.50
XE421	MTWTF	1600	1640	£16.50
Hawarden (Chester)–Rhoose				
XE404	MTWTF	0900	0940	£16.50
XE422	MTWTF	1700	1740	£16.50
Rhoose–Brest				
XE709	TT	1100	1210	£30.50
Brest–Rhoose				
XE712	TT	1300	1410	£30.50
Rhoose–Cherbourg				
XE309	MWF	1100	1200	£30.50
Cherbourg–Rhoose				
XE312	MWF	1300	1400	£30.50

In the spring of 1978, Air Wales' second aircraft, a new Brazilian-built, nineteen-passenger Embraer EMB-110 Bandeirante G-CELT was delivered to Rhoose and inaugurated a new daily Rhoose to Brussels scheduled service. Air Wales established an inter-line agreement with Brussels-based Sabena, which meant that many passengers using the Rhoose–Brussels service were connecting to Sabena's vast worldwide network. Capt. John Evans was the Director of Operations and in a *Western Mail* interview in January 1978 said, 'The initial weeks have been better than expected. I estimated that in the first year we would carry about 4,000 passengers on the north-south route, but on present patterns this could be about 5,000'. Capt. E. Meddings was Air Wales' chief pilot and Ivan Ulic, a Yugoslavian, was one of the first captains to join Air Wales – Meddings and Ulic ferried the airline's new Bandeirante from Sao Paulo, Brazil, to Rhoose. Other Air Wales staff included Terry Fox, who had worked for Brymon Airways and IAS Cargo as operations officer; Linda Thomas, a former Cambrian Airways employee; David Parsons, the senior duty officer; and Colin Lewis, the reservations supervisor, a former Air Rhodesia employee. The airline was also optimistic that the new Ford plant opened at Bridgend would generate not only extra passengers but also extra air freight.

There was considerable discussion about a proposed Swansea–Rhoose–London Gatwick service, but Air Wales, other than an occasional charter, never inaugurated schedules from Swansea. For the summer of 1978 Air Wales ensured that Chester passengers (or Clwyd as it was now known) could connect at Rhoose with the Cherbourg service which routed via Bournemouth, expanding the destinations served from Chester. The Cherbourg service was sold as a quick way for Welsh passengers to get to Paris, linking at Cherbourg to the SNCF 'Turbo-Train' via Caen to Paris.

Air Wales'
Embraer EMB.110
Bandeirante
G-CELT was used
to inaugurate the
airline's schedule
from Rhoose to
Brussels in spring
1978. (Geoff Jones)

The new airport committee chairman, Hayden J. Tabram, speaking at the same time and following the airport's rebranding as Cardiff (Wales) Airport, was also optimistic, saying, 'I have high hopes for Air Wales and the airport's future – Welsh holidaymakers must keep faith with Cardiff (Wales) Airport as there are now sixty-three holiday destinations in seven countries which people can fly to from the airport'. Other Air Wales services were from Rhoose to Bournemouth, Bordeaux and Dinard, plus one to London (Gatwick). However, before the airline's second Bandeirante (G-BGNK) could be delivered, Air Wales ceased operations on 6 April 1979 – a press release from David King, Air Wales' chairman announced on 2 April the cessation of the Rhoose to Brussels service on 6 April, 'because after months of talks Welsh financial involvement and discussions with other airlines had regrettably come to nought – our forecasts indicate about a further 15 months before this service becomes profitable'. The north–south Wales service was to continue as normal, plus the prospect of three daily rotations on Monday, Wednesday and Friday, but on 30 June G-BAVM, another Navajo Chieftain Air Wales was using, arrived at Rhoose at 1726hrs on the final service from Hawarden, then departed empty to Coventry. Air Wales' sole operational Bandeirante went to Fairflight Charters/Air Ecosse and the assets and routes were taken over by British & Commonwealth Shipping from 1 January 1980, as part of the formation of Air UK.

Inter European Airways

Based at Rhoose, but with its head office in Cardiff city centre, the airline was founded in 1987 by the Aspro family of local businessmen, well known for their chain of travel agencies and as tour operators, Aspro Travel and Aspro Holidays. Inter European Airways' (IEA) first aircraft was a Boeing 737-200 leased from GPA, and as well as their operations from Rhoose, they also flew from Bristol, and later Belfast and Manchester. They then acquired two brand new Boeing 737-300s (G-BNGL and 'GM), again leased from GPA, for the 1988 summer season of flights to Malaga, Palma, Corfu, Larnaca, Faro, Pisa, Milan and Thessalonika. The airline grew under the guidance of former British Airways chief pilot and now Inter European Director of Flight Operations, Bob Seed. Their next acquisition was two leased Boeing 757-200s, but in 1992 Bob Seed was replaced by ex-Air Europe Chief Pilot Alan Dix, and with the change a large influx of unemployed ex-Air Europe pilots then followed. The airline then took the decision to acquire Airbus A320 family aircraft, introduced in 1993, but shortly afterwards the airline was taken over by Airtours International (not to be confused with BEA Airtours) and the head office switched from Cardiff to Manchester.

Busy ramp scene at Rhoose in September 1992 with aircraft from three of the airport's stalwart airlines: Inter European, Airtours and Britannia. (Geoff Jones)

179 expectant passengers seated aboard Airtours Airbus A320 G-SUEE ready for their holiday flight from Rhoose to Las Palmas in March 1997. (Geoff Jones)

Some of Airtours' large fleet of McDonnell Douglas MD-83s were based at Rhoose. Pictured is G-GMJM at push-back in September 1992. (Geoff Jones)

Taxiing for departure at Rhoose in August 1995, an Airtours Airbus A320, G-YJBM. (Geoff Jones)

Launch of Airtours' direct flights from Rhoose to Orlando, Florida on 1 May 1998, using a leased Boeing 747-200. (Cardiff Airport)

An important operations base at Rhoose continued, with services flown by Airtours' eight-strong fleet of leased McDonnell Douglas MD-83s, but these were slowly replaced by Airbus A320 family aircraft. However, Rhoose was no longer the main base, and the engineering division that had been formed there was dispensed with. For the 1998 season Airtours leased an Air New Zealand Boeing 747-200 (ZK-NZZ) for direct services from Rhoose to Orlando, Florida. Amongst much razzmatazz, including a Dixieland jazz band on the apron, the 747 in basic Air New Zealand colours but with Airtours titles and logo on the tail positioned in from Manchester on the morning of 1 May as the AIH 51, before departing to Orlando with a full load of Disney-bound holidaymakers. It was based at Rhoose until 23 October, but on 15 May had to be substituted with Corsair Boeing 747-312 F-GSUN, which positioned in from Paris Orly. Airtours changed its name to MyTravel Airways on 1 February 2002, but the following year got into serious financial problems (they had tried to start up a low-fares unit called MyTravel Lite) and was saved from collapse by a merger with Thomas Cook. Throughout these machinations Airbus A320 and A321 flights continued from Rhoose, with the occasional A330 rotation as well.

Air Wales No.2

This airline was formed by aviation brokers IAG and a consortium of Welsh businessmen headed by reclusive Swansea property financier Roy Thomas. John Evans, who was with the first Air Wales, was at the helm for the airline's day-to-day operations, which commenced on 6 October 2000 using a Dornier Do.228 for a thrice-weekly Rhoose to Cork service. The airline's original plan was to start services on St David's Day in 2000, flying an EMB-110 Bandeirante based at the former wartime airfield at Pembrey (near Llanelli), which had recently been reopened. Charter services were to be offered followed by a scheduled service to link to London Stansted, where the low-fare airlines Ryanair, Go and easyJet were burgeoning and changing airline history. This was delayed with a June 2000 launch proposed on the Haverfordwest–Pembrey–Rhoose–Stansted route. Haverfordwest and Pembrey airports proved unsuitable at the time for scheduled operations, so the Rhoose–Cork service was launched as an alternative. Other routes from Rhoose to Manchester, and Rhoose–Shoreham (Brighton)–

Above First Dornier Do228 G-BUXT acquired by Air Wales taxiing here at Rhoose in July 2001. (Geoff Jones)

Right Two of Air Wales' fleet of five ATR-42 turboprops. (Geoff Jones)

Pontoise (Paris) were discussed and an Ayres-built LET L-610 turboprop was demonstrated to the airline in spring 2000 at Rhoose. No order followed and neither did these services.

Swansea Airport was the next option for Air Wales as its base and, with the support of Korean automotive group Daewoo, the airline arranged the lease of a second Dornier Do.228 to commence Swansea to Dublin and Cork schedules in October 2001. One of Air Wales' Do.228s was based at Rhoose and began a twice-daily service to Manchester, but this ceased on 30 August 2001 due to poor load factors. Issues at Swansea resulted in the airline's decision to centralise operations and line maintenance at Rhoose and in autumn 2002 the two Dorniers were replaced by two Beech 1900Ds leased from German airline Avanti Air and used on the schedules from Rhoose to Cork and Dublin. In March 2003 Air Wales' first ATR-42 was delivered and used for services to Ireland and Jersey, plus a short-lived Swansea–Rhoose–London City service. By 2004 Air Wales had a fleet of five Rhoose-based ATR-42s, was operating a hub at Plymouth City Airport and in February signed an agreement with bmibaby to operate that airline's schedules from Rhoose to Belfast, Cork and Glasgow (Prestwick), routes that could not support a Boeing 737-300. A Rhoose–Jersey service for bmibaby soon followed, in September 2004 a new service from Rhoose to Aberdeen via Liverpool was also inaugurated and in October routes from Norwich to Dublin and Rhoose. The bmibaby partnership at Rhoose grew and in December 2004 Air Wales commenced flying routes from Rhoose to Paris (Charles de Gaulle) and to Durham Tees Valley. Air Wales' fleet grew to five ATR-42s, they employed nearly 200 staff and in the last six months of 2004 the airline grew by 34 per cent. However, expansion came at a cost with a pre-tax loss of £3.9 million in the twelve months to March 2004 – in the same period revenues rose from £2.7 to £5.9 million. The Welsh dragon was flying high again but this was to be short lived with continuing and unsustainable losses. In December 2005 there was a 'fall-out' with bmibaby and the airline also abandoned scheduled services from Plymouth in February 2006.

On 23 April all scheduled services from Rhoose were also abandoned and eighty employees there lost their jobs. With Air Wales' AOC (Air Operators Certificate) still valid and retaining two of their ATR-42s, they chartered aircraft out, including to Guernsey-based Aurigny Air Services, but after a year were wound up completely. Other airlines quickly jumped in and commenced services on the better routes that Air Wales had established from Rhoose, Aer Arann to Cork, Eastern to Newcastle, bmibaby to Jersey, Air Southwest to Plymouth and Newquay, and flybe to Belfast and Paris.

Airways International Cymru

A bold venture at Rhoose at the height of the IT (inclusive tour) boom in the 1970s and 1980s, Airways International Cymru (AIC) was a logical progression by Tony Clemo from his Church Street, Cardiff-based Red Dragon Travel. Tony Clemo was a well-known local businessman, owner of a city night club and Director of Cardiff City Football Club. He had learnt to fly at Cambrian Flying Club in the 1970s, a club he subsequently bought. After qualifying for his private pilot's licence and gaining a twin rating, he bought his own light aircraft, a Piper Aerostar G-MOVE. With this experience he figured that instead of chartering other airlines to fly his customers to popular Mediterranean holiday destinations, why not form your own airline and keep everything in-house?

AIC was formed in October 1983, acquired an ex-Quebecair BAC1-11 jet (G-YMRU) and leased another, G-AXMU, from British Island Airways. AIC picked up IT charter work at several UK airports and, using the radio call-sign identity *Welshair*, flew its first service in February 1984 and first holiday flight from Rhoose for Red Dragon Travel in April. The former Cambrian headquarters, 'the white house', was used as the airline's headquarters and with BAC1-11s in the fleet, the airline hired many redundant Cambrian and Laker Airways personnel who were familiar with the type. Later in 1984 AIC acquired another ex-Quebecair BAC1-11 G-WLAD and returned G-AXMU to BIA – Aerostar G-MOVE was also enlisted to act as a crew ferry aircraft. With business booming in 1985 and regular flights from Bristol as well, a Boeing 737-200 G-BAZI was leased from GPA (Guinness Peat Aviation) and then, with the BAC1-11s uneconomic and disposed of, for the 1986 summer season a Boeing 737-300 (G-PROC) was leased with a second Boeing 737-300 (G-PROK) soon after. In 1987 a new Boeing 737-300 G-BNCT was leased from ILFC (International Lease Finance Corp), but after the summer season one of the 737s was leased on to an airline in the US. Difficulties regarding the contract and lack of payments for the lease led to financial difficulties at AIC, and in early 1988 the airline's aircraft were repossessed by their leasers or mortgagees. AIC ceased operations in 1988, having regularly served twenty different European holiday destinations during its four years of operations at Rhoose.

However, Tony Clemo's airline aspirations didn't die with AIC and within a few weeks he had set up a new airline at Rhoose, Diamond Airways, with the Boeing 737-200 G-BAZI and using the ICAO three-letter flight code designator DMD – he also used other 737s G-BOSA and G-BKMS. Their first reported flight was to Luton on 25 March, then on 12 April to Toulouse. Other flights, mostly from Rhoose, were spasmodic in the next few months, again to Toulouse, to Forli, Venice and Rome Ciampino in Italy, then flights from Manchester to Izmir, Mykonos and Athens on 13 May. There were issues about the name 'Diamond' so the airline's name was changed to Amber Air, although the tail logo was retained. The last reported flight by the airline was on 22 June 1988, when G-BOSA was noted at Heathrow flying Alitalia schedules during an Alitalia strike.

Right G-YMRU, one
of two BAC1-11s that
Airways Cymru used
to start operations, in
March 1987. (Geoff
Jones)

Below Airways Cymru's
Boeing 737-200
G-BAZI on stand 12
at Rhoose in January
1987. (Geoff Jones)

Picking up the pieces
from the demise of
Airways Cymru, Amberair
(initially Diamond
Airways) was a short-lived
Rhoose-based charter
airline in November 1988.
(Mike Kemp)

Manx Airlines

This Isle of Man-based airline's first connection with Wales and Rhoose was its June 1987 lease of the Airways International Cymru BAC1-11 G-WLAD to fly their schedules between the Isle of Man (Ronaldsway) and London Heathrow pending delivery of their first BAe146 on 30 November. Expanding their route map, Manx's summer 1991 schedules featured Rhoose for the first time, a daily return service from the Isle of Man to Jersey via Dublin and Rhoose operated by a BAe ATP turboprop. Passenger figures from Rhoose were exceptionally good, and this prompted Manx's far-sighted managing director Terry Liddiard to investigate opening a new hub for the airline at Rhoose. Applications were made to the CAA for eight new scheduled routes from Rhoose to Paris, Brussels, Düsseldorf, Belfast, Dublin, Manchester, Jersey and Belfast. Approval for all of these routes was given, except Manchester, with a March 1991 start date, with Paris waiting until October. Manx said at the time: 'Cardiff-Wales Airport is regarded as the finest airport west of London and the authorities welcomed the initiative of Manx Airlines to bring new routes and business to the airport.'

As Manx was now to operate outside the jurisdiction of the Isle of Man, it had to create a British-based company to satisfy EU regulations. Manx Airlines (Europe) Ltd was formed and registered in March 1991 at Donington Hall as a subsidiary of Airlines of Britain Holdings plc, whose chairman was Michael Bishop from bmi. Manx had already realised that specialist new aircraft would be required at Rhoose for their new hub services and ordered two BAe Jetstream 31s in a special sixteen-seat configuration, appropriately registered G-GLAM and G-WENT, delivered in time for the inauguration of services at Rhoose on 25 March 1991. Mike Vickers became the Manx station manager at Rhoose, supported by Charlotte Kosh who had to recruit and train a new team of cabin staff for the Jetstreams as well as looking after catering. Rai Watts joined Manx to become regional sales manager for Manx in South Wales and the surrounding regions. The new services were generally successful, although loads on the Düsseldorf route were disappointing and it was dropped. More capacity was required as traffic built, and additional rotations were scheduled for the Rhoose to Belfast and Glasgow services until the orders for larger Jetstream 41s was placed, the first of five, G-WAWR delivered to Rhoose in February 1993. Manx, along with Loganair in Scotland, were the launch customers for the new twenty-nine-seat J41s – the other J41s that would be based at Rhoose were G-WAWL, 'YR, 'ND and 'FT.

Celebrating Manx Airlines' first anniversary at Rhoose in spring 1992 with Cardiff operations manager Rai Watts (left), stewardess Katherine Ham and travel agent Jim Strachan. (Geoff Jones Collection)

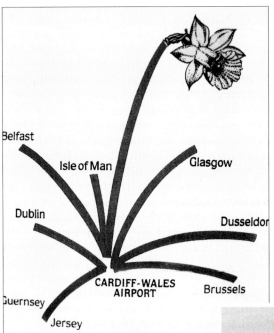

Manx Airlines route system from Rhoose (Cardiff–Wales) in summer 1991. (Geoff Jones Collection)

Rhoose's scheduled services burgeoned in the 1990s largely thanks to Manx, then British Airways Express and Regional – three Jetstream 41s in the colours of BA Express are seen here in August 1996. (Geoff Jones)

Above left Two thirds of the Derby Airways Argonaut fleet on a busy summer Friday in 1964 (Geoff Jones). *Below left* Derby Airways Argonaut G-ALHS in 1964 in front of what was then considered a suitable security fence. (Geoff Jones)

By 1994 Manx was flying to nine destinations from Rhoose and, system-wide, was carrying 1.729 million passengers; it had an overall staff of 800 and operated twenty-four aircraft. However, at the end of the year it was announced that the airline was to become a British Airways franchise, so during 1995 the Rhoose-based Jetstream 41s started to appear in the BA livery, and the cabin crew and ground staff were wearing BA uniforms. The BA Union Jack colours were back at Rhoose operating scheduled services after a break of fifteen years. British Regional also took the decision to order fifteen of the Brazilian-built regional jets, fifty-seat Embraer ERJ145s. These regional jets were delivered between June 1997 and March 2000, being gradually integrated in to British Regional's schedules, including those at Rhoose. Change was imminent though – at Rhoose new lower fares were introduced by Manx on the Dublin route (due to competition from Ryanair) but most significantly in September there was a change of name from Manx Airlines (Europe) Ltd to British Regional Airlines Ltd (BRAL), plus the June 1998 decision to float the company on the London stock exchange. On 8 March 2001 British Airways agreed to purchase BRAL for £78 million, including Manx, Brymon and British Airways Regional (CityFlyer and Loganair joined later) to form British Airways CitiExpress, with the 'World Image' tail colours of British Airways a common sight at Rhoose, along with the last of the J41s – services at Rhoose were abandoned between January and March 2003. The last Belfast City flights were flown by ERJ145 G-EMBV on the 3rd, by Jetstream 41 G-MAJD on the 4th and the final flight by a DHC-8 G-BRYX on 5 January – the last Jersey flight was ERJ145 G-ERJC on the 4th and the same aircraft flew the last Brussels service on 5 January. Paris services continued until 28 March, with three daily flights all operated by ERJ145 G-EMBY. Bmibaby took over many of these routes and services. In February 2006 BA CitiExpress was rebranded as BA Connect and in November was acquired by flybe (in which BA still has a 15 per cent shareholding).

In 2010 flybe was Rhoose's third most important carrier in terms of passengers but largest in terms of aircraft movements, using its fleet of seventy-eight-seat, Canadian-built Bombardier DHC-8 Dash 400 turboprops – and occasionally Embraer E.195 jets – to fly schedules to Belfast City, Edinburgh, Glasgow and Paris CDG. Flybe had appeared at Rhoose in its earlier guise of Jersey European Airways (JEA) when it was flying DHC-6 Twin Otters on passenger schedules in 1985 and 1986, and then on night-time cargo/mail flights. Flybe recommenced operations at Rhoose on 29 April 2007, and continues to grow its Welsh operation here.

Bmibaby

Bmibaby is the latest manifestation of British independent airline Derby Airways. As Derby Aviation the airline operated its first scheduled passenger service on 18 July 1953, a Dragon Rapide flight from Derby (Burnaston) via Wolverhampton to Jersey. Derby Airways was registered as an airline in March 1959 having acquired Dakotas and Miles Marathon aircraft (see Chapter 6). The airline's aircraft, Douglas DC-3s G-AMSW and 'SX first landed at Rhoose in December 1958 before the 31 May 1960 inauguration of the airline's first schedule from Rhoose to Palma, Majorca. In 1963 these Palma services were operated by one or more of the three Canadair C-4 Argonaut aircraft Derby Airways had bought. On 1 October 1964 the airline changed its name to British Midland Airways (BMA) and much later, in 2001, to British Midland International (BMI) – it is from this name that the airline's low-fare unit bmibaby, 'The Airline With Tiny Fares', was formed in 2002, establishing its first hub at East Midland Airport and flying its first schedule to Malaga on 20 March. Bmibaby's second hub was opened at Rhoose on 25 October with two Boeing 737-300s based to fly schedules to nine destinations in the UK and Europe. Bmibaby's arrival at Rhoose was the catalyst for British Airways subsidiary BA CitiExpress to announce its withdrawal of scheduled passenger services from Rhoose.

On the occasion of bmibaby's first anniversary of starting operations at Rhoose they had carried almost three-quarters of a million passengers and embraced their Welsh base

Bmibaby's two Rhoose-based Boeing 737-300s in February 2003. (Geoff Jones)

by painting Boeing 737-500 G-BVKD in a special Wales Tourist Board colour scheme with images of the Welsh hills, a 'Free Duty' slogan and 'visitwales.com' on its tail. Their winter 2003/04 timetable showed services to thirteen destinations from Rhoose, to Alicante, Belfast International, Cork, Edinburgh, Geneva (once a week), Glasgow Prestwick, Jersey, Malaga, Milan Bergamo (once a week), Palma, Paris, Prague and Toulouse (once a week). In the meantime, they had also opened hubs at Manchester and Teesside. Some of these services were operated for bmibaby by Air Wales ATR 42s (see page 54)

Through ups and downs, bmibaby continued to serve Wales and its airport at Rhoose – bmi became 80 per cent owned by Germany's Lufthansa in October 2008 and a wholly owned subsidiary by November 2009, but despite many rumours and counter-rumours, by the end of 2010 bmibaby was still a major player at Rhoose with two 737-based and scheduled services to twelve destinations, new ones from the 2003 list above being Faro, Ibiza, Mahon (Menorca), Murcia and Munich. They were also the second largest operator at Rhoose in 2010 in terms of passenger numbers, behind TUI and ahead of flybe.

However, on 13 April 2011 the news broke that bmibaby were to pull out of Rhoose (and Manchester) at the end of the summer 2011 flying schedule. Sixty-nine staff (forty-four cabin crew, twenty-four pilots and one manager) were employed at Rhoose at the time of the announcement, and were offered the opportunity to redeploy to the Midlands (East Midlands and Birmingham). At the time of the announcement bmibaby was flying services from Rhoose to nine destinations, Geneva, Faro, Belfast City, Malaga, Murcia, Alicante, Ibiza, Palma and Mahon. Simultaneously the airline announced seven new routes from George Best Belfast City Airport.

6

OTHER SCHEDULES, CHARTERS AND AIR FREIGHT

Thanks to a detailed study of the Rhoose movements log for some of the early years of commercial operations (1959 to 1961) by Tony Merton-Jones (current editor of *Propliner* magazine) a variety of airline operations are revealed, both scheduled and charter, that contrast with the apparent, current paucity. As well as the scheduled operations of Cambrian Airways and Aer Lingus, charters were fairly numerous.

Derby Airways put in their first appearances at Rhoose on 29 and 31 December 1958 with DC-3 flights with G-AMSW, 'MSX and 'NTD to their base at Burnaston (Derby) and Edinburgh Turnhouse. On 21 July 1959 their DC-3 G-ANTD arrived at Rhoose from Tarbes in south-west France before flying back to its base at Burnaston. The airline provided a rare treat at Rhoose on 9 August 1959 when their Miles M.60 Marathon G-AMHR *Monsal Dale* arrived, flying a delayed late-night service from Jersey to Bournemouth (Hurn) but stopping at Rhoose at 2153hrs because the customs facilities at Hurn had closed – it then departed at 2227hrs to Gloucester (Staverton) and on to its home base at Burnaston. From 1960 Derby Airways inaugurated a raft of DC-3 services from Rhoose to Luxembourg, Nice, Perpignan and Ostend. It was two years later, in 1962, that Derby Airways started another schedule from Rhoose, flying with DC-3s via Bristol to Palma, Majorca. Inclusive tour (IT) charters from Rhoose to Palma continued in 1963 with both DC-3s and the airline's four-engine Canadair C-4 Argonauts that they had acquired in October 1961. The thrill of seeing the relatively small apron at Rhoose with up to three of these behemoths flying IT charters cannot be easily described. On 30 July 1964 it was announced that Derby Airways was to change its name to British Midland Airways (BMA). By summer 1965 BMA had acquired its first turboprops, a Handley Page HPR.7 Herald (G-ASKK) and Viscounts – the airline's Rhoose timetable showed Friday and Monday Argonaut flights via Bristol to Palma, Majorca with connecting flights from Palma to Barcelona, and DC-3s were flying four times a week to Ostend (again via Bristol). Whilst the Herald was mainly used for BMI flights from the new East Midlands Airport at Castle Donington, Luton and Gloucester to Jersey and Guernsey, it did occasionally substitute for DC-3s at Rhoose. In the 1965 timetable the fares quoted included a single from Rhoose to Palma at £27 3s and return £51 12s – Ostend was £17 14s return – all flights having a free baggage weight allowance of 15kg.

Dan-Air's first appearance at Rhoose was operating a charter flight on Sunday 13 March 1960 following the Wales *v.* Ireland rugby international in Dublin. Amongst the chartered BKS and Derby Airways DC-3s, Dan-Air's G-AMSU appeared, along with their DC-3 G-AMSS the following day. In 1959 Dan-Air, formed in March 1953 as a subsidiary of Davies & Newman Ltd shipping brokers, successfully bid for a licence to fly a scheduled service from both Bristol and

British Midland's first turboprop aircraft was the HPR.7 Herald G-ASKK which visited Rhoose soon after the airline acquired it in February 1965. (Geoff Jones)

Dan-Air had a large fleet of HS748 twin-turboprops. G-ARAY is on stand 12 in the summer of 1987, an Airways Cymru BAC1-11 beyond. (Geoff Jones)

Dan-Air's, and the UK's, sole Nord 262 G-AYFR replaced DC-3s and operated the Link-City services from 22 July 1970. (Mike Kemp)

Dan-Air BAC1-11 G-AXCK operating a charter c.1970. (Kelvin Lumb)

Rhoose following the opening of Bristol's new airport at Lulsgate. They acquired two DH.104 Doves G-AIWF and G-ALVF – in May 1960 a new Rhoose/Bristol service to the Isle of Man was inaugurated using the Doves, followed on 16 July 1960 by the airline's first international scheduled service from Rhoose/Bristol to Basle in Switzerland using DC-3 G-AMSU, flown on this inaugural flight by a Capt. Davies. Also on 16 July Dan-Air extended its 'Link-City' Liverpool–Bristol–Rhoose service to include Plymouth using Doves and DC-3s. Many airlines were looking for the enigmatic 'DC-3 replacement' – having looked at the BN-2 Islander, DHC-6 Twin Otter, Beechcraft 99 and Handley Page Jetstream, in 1970 Dan-Air introduced an unusual new type, the French-built, twenty-nine-passenger Nord 262, acquired in June from Air Ceylon and becoming G-AYFR. It entered service on 22 July, despite some passenger resistance from a few DC-3 lovers, flying the Link-City service from Newcastle to Bristol via Liverpool and Rhoose, regularly achieving five-minute turnarounds at intermediate stops such as Rhoose. The same day that the Nord 262 entered service the airline's venerable DC-3 G-AMPP was retired. A few days later Dan-Air's last DC-3, G-AMSU, which had become a regular at Rhoose, was flown to the airline's base at Lasham, Hampshire, for preservation. The Nord 262 flew its last service for Dan-Air on 21 January 1972, the airline having decided to invest in a pair of larger-capacity, fifty-seat Avro 748 (subsequently HS.748) aircraft. When Dan-Air acquired Skyways International in 1972 a further four HS.748s joined their fleet, all of them at one time or another visiting Rhoose.

The Link-City service from Rhoose continued with HS.748s for many years and in 1974 Dan-Air started using the HS.748 on the Rhoose to Amsterdam service via Bristol, and by 1977 was flying 41,000 passengers a year from Rhoose. As Dan-Air expanded they acquired a variety of airliners, including the Viscount, BAC1-11, Boeing 727, DH Comet IV and, from May 1988, onwards the Boeing 737-300. All of these visited Rhoose on a variety of operations, mainly charter flights (for Global of London Ltd, Cambrian Air Holidays, Hourmont Travel and Schools Abroad). They built a significant base at Rhoose and by 1978 had six traffic staff and four reservations staff looking after Dan-Air's seven scheduled services, including former BA services. British Airways ceased passenger schedules at Rhoose in 1980, operating the last of Cambrian's former schedules with the dwindling Viscount fleet. Dan-Air stepped in to operate these schedules, which included Rhoose to Belfast, Dublin, Guernsey, Jersey and Paris and, in the early 1980s, Dan-Air had three or four HS.748s based at Rhoose.

The Link-City concept was further developed in 1982 when Metropolitan Airways, a subsidiary of Alderney Air Ferries (Holdings) Ltd, began operating under the Link-City name with a pair of Twin Otters, G-BELS and 'HFD. The aircraft were in full Dan-Air colours with 'Dan-Air Link City' scribed over the entry door – Metropolitan provided the aircraft, but Dan-Air the reservations and other facilities. These were flown on services between Bournemouth, Rhoose, Bristol, Birmingham, Manchester, Leeds/Bradford and Glasgow. In May 1983 Dan-Air became the first airline to put the four-engine British Aerospace BAe146 into commercial service and in the summer of 1984 the type was a regular at Rhoose flying the 'round-robin' schedule to Jersey, Guernsey and back to Bristol and Rhoose. This was part of a thirteen-hour, eleven-sector day for the hard-worked BAe146, with an average block time of forty-three minutes and average turnaround time at each stop of only fifteen minutes. I remember travelling several times from Rhoose with Dan-Air on this 146 service to the Channel Islands and it was always full, a fact confirmed by the airline's increased passenger figures. Metropolitan Airways Link-City operation for Dan-Air operated until 31 August 1985, when Metropolitan Airways suspended services and went into liquidation. Brown Air took over the Glasgow route (see later in chapter). A similar arrangement for services from Rhoose and Bristol to Glasgow was agreed between Dan-Air and Centreline using a pair of EMB-110 Bandeirantes for a short period in October 1982. On 23 October 1992 Dan-Air ceased operations, some of its schedules – mainly from London Gatwick – and assets being sold to BA.

Most notable airliner visitors in the late 1950s and early 1960s were those of the Scandinavian airlines Braathens, Widerøe's, Transair and Fred Olsen, many of these operating 'sailors charters', delivering and picking up ships' crews from the South Wales ports. More parochial, yet, with the hindsight of over fifty years, eclectic, were visits from many of the UK's other independent airlines: British Westpoint (Dragon Rapides and DC-3) Olley Air Services (Dragon Rapide), Morton Air Services (Doves and Herons), Orion Airways (Viking), Air Safaris and Overseas Aviation (all Vikings), Channel Airways (Dove), Silver City (DC-3), Mercury Airlines (DC-3) and Tyne Tees (Dove). Other foreign airlines whose aircraft made appearances at Rhoose in the early 1960s were Seven Seas Airlines from the USA (DC-4), Iberia (CV440) EC-AMR and Sudflug from Germany (Heron) D-CASE. This period demonstrated the transition by many smaller airlines from use of older war-surplus types such as the DH.89 Dragon Rapide to the more modern commuter types, such as the DH Dove and Heron. (See Appendix 1 for a full list of airlines that have used Rhoose.)

A further few details are useful to describe the operations by the Scandinavian airlines mentioned above. In 1946 the Norwegian shipping line Fred Olsen formed an airline subsidiary that operated until closed in 1997. Fred Olsen Air Transport started operations using two Douglas DC-3s and three Douglas C-47s. The first record of a Fred Olsen DC-3 arriving in the principality was in June 1949, when two positioned from Belfast after dropping off a ship's crew and 'flew on to Wales' (presumably Cardiff, but whether Pengam, Llandow or Rhoose isn't known) to collect the Norwegian Ladies' Choir, who were then flown home to Oslo. Other ship crew charters were flown to 'Cardiff' in June and July 1950. In summer 1955 Fred Olsen DC-3s visited Rhoose on several occasions. On 19 July 1956 DC-3 LN-IAS flew a charter from Oslo to Rhoose and on to Southend – the airline was flying almost daily between Oslo and Southend in summer 1956. On 7 September the same aircraft flew eleven passengers on a Cardiff–Southend–Jarlsberg service and was back in South Wales again on 19 September to fly from Rhoose to Stavanger via Southend. Summer 1957 was the last full year of DC-3 operations by Fred Olsen, the airline acquiring turboprop Viscounts and three Curtiss C-46 Commandos; LN-NAB and LN-IAS made several flights to Rhoose during July and August, many of them via Southend. Also, on 27 March 1959 DC-3 LN-IAS made a six-hour and two-minute direct flight from Oslo to Rhoose, returning to Oslo the next day – this aircraft was back again on 9 June. The first Fred Olsen C-46 Commando visit to Rhoose was LN-FOR, used primarily as a freighter, which touched down on 21 April 1959 inbound from Oslo and departed the next day, also to Oslo. Then Rhoose had its first visit by a Fred Olsen Viscount, LN-FOI, flying passengers from Kristiansand on Saturday 7 May, touching down at 1233hrs and leaving the following afternoon for Oslo – another rotation to Rhoose from Rotterdam on 30 May saw Viscount LN-FOI back again, and on 11 October this aircraft flew in from Stavanger and back again, recorded in the airport's movement log as a Scandinavian Airline Systems (SAS) flight. On 1 July 1961 Viscount LN-FOK arrived from Torp and this Viscount visited Rhoose twice again during July, on 22nd from Southend before continuing to Palma and on 24 July, flying from Southend and back to Oslo.

A DC-3 LN-PAS of another Norwegian airline, Braathens SAFE, touched down at Rhoose from Stavanger on 7 December 1960, before returning the same day; this airline operated several more flights in July 1961 with their DC-3s LN-PAS and LN-SUK from Stavanger and Kristiansand. Visits by yet another Norwegian-based airline to Rhoose, Widerøe's Flyveselskap, were noted on 29 August 1963 when their new Nord 260 Super Broussard LN-LMB touched down, followed the next year on 28 February by their DC-3 LN-RTA. On 13 July 1961 Braathen's Douglas DC-4 LN-SUP arrived from Southend, and several years later, on 26 January 1965, made another appearance. Braathens SAFE was founded by Ludwig G. Braathen and commenced operations at Oslo's Fornebu Airport in January 1947, becoming Norway's foremost domestic airline, but also from 1960 operating extensive charter flights – it survived until 2004 until it merged with Scandinavian Airlines Norway and became SAS Braathens.

These Scandinavian charters were still part of the Rhoose scene up until 1965, but then on 27 March 1970 the arrival of Fred Olsen Convair 340 LN-FOF on a passenger charter from Gothenburg revived old memories. In addition, the sight of a Convair at Rhoose was a rarity as it departed on a round trip to Gatwick the following day and was back again at Rhoose on

At dusk on 22 July 1965 Capitol Airways Curtiss C-46 N9890Z arrived from London Heathrow. (Geoff Jones)

One of the Scandinavian airlines to visit Rhoose regularly was Oslo-based Fred Olsen, its DC-3 LN-IAS seen here on the Rhoose apron alongside an Aer Lingus DC-3 and Cambrian Dove in 1959. (Robert C. Thursby)

Blackbushe-based Orion Airways Viking G-AHOS, one of three in their fleet, makes a rare visit *c.*1958. (Robert C. Thursby)

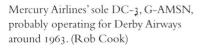

Mercury Airlines' sole DC-3, G-AMSN, probably operating for Derby Airways around 1963. (Rob Cook)

Fred Olsen Convair CV-340 LN-FOV at Rhoose in March 1970, one of many Scandinavian aircraft that operated charter flights to and from Rhoose. (Adrian Balch Collection)

Polish airline LOT flew the Welsh National Youth Orchestra to Dresden in Ilyushin IL-18 SP-LSI in 1980. (Geoff Jones)

A turboprop conversion, this picture shows Convair CV-580 LN-BWN (formerly with Partnair A/S) of Norwegian charter airline Nor-Fly on 1 August 1981. (Geoff Jones)

30 March for an evening return flight to Gothenburg. And there was to be one further episode of Scandinavian 'magic' at Rhoose on 1 August 1981, when the Honefoss, Norway-based charter operator Nor-Fly A/S operated one of a series of charters to Norway with its smart turbo-powered Convair 580 LN-BWN. Another memorable Convair 'event' at Rhoose coincided with the BBC's *It's An International Knock Out* being held in the grounds of Cardiff Castle on 5 August 1970 (see Chapter 7).

On 26 February 1959 probably the first Curtiss C-46 Commander to be seen at Rhoose, N4086A registered to the Smith Aircraft Corporation, arrived from Blackbushe at 1119hrs and departed back to this Hampshire airfield at 1231hrs. The Fred Olsen C-46 visits have already been detailed but on 5 June 1960 another Scandinavian airline, Transair, flew their C-46 SE-CFF to Rhoose from Jersey and then onwards to Southend. Curtiss C-46 Commander N9890Z of US airline Capitol – one of several on lease to Lufthansa at the time – was a welcome arrival from London Heathrow on the evening of 22 July 1965. On 20 August 1966 two other classic 'prop-liners' arrived, this time Royal Canadian Air Force Bristol B170 Freighters (9699 and 9850) carrying horses for the Royal Canadian Mounted Police who were giving a display as part of the Floodlight Tattoo in Cardiff Castle. In 1981 the Cardiff Searchlight Tattoo attracted the Oman State Police Band who arrived in Boeing 727-30 A40-CF between 6 and 8, then 13 and 15 August.

Cambrian's BAC1-11 pilots were trained initially by Autair, an expanding Luton-based scheduled and charter operator. On 1 January 1970 Autair officially became Court Line, with seven new BAC1-11 srs500s delivered at the time that IT charters to Mediterranean resorts were burgeoning (see image, p151). From April 1970 onwards, Court Line started flying BAC1-11 flights from Rhoose to Alicante, Gerona, Ibiza, Palma, Rimini and Venice. Everyone remembers Court Line's garishly coloured aircraft, the stylish and colourful uniforms of the flight attendants – and their hemlines – and how quickly the company grew and capitalised on the fast-growing market. They were flying passengers on behalf of Clarksons Holidays, a huge tour operator at the time which took over Cardiff-based Hourmont Holidays. As well as the BAC1-11s, the airline used a Piper PA-31 Navajo Chieftain G-AYEI and Bell Jet Ranger helicopter for crew ferry between Rhoose and their Luton base. Expanding rapidly, Court Line added two Lockheed L1011 Tristars to its fleet in 1973, partly to service its growing holiday empire in the Caribbean, but also to fly 400 passengers at a time from Gatwick and Luton to

One of two Royal Canadian Air Force Bristol Freighters that flew Royal Canadian Mounted Police horses to Rhoose for the Cardiff International Floodlight Tattoo on 20 August 1966. (Geoff Jones)

Mediterranean resorts. By the summer of 1974 Court Line's financial situation was suffering from the economic downturn and poor bookings. On 15 August the airline collapsed and most of its aircraft returned to Luton. However, BAC1-11 G-AYOR was impounded at Rhoose because of unpaid landing fees – Court Line's demise was at the time the worst of any airline in the history of British aviation with 50,000 passengers left stranded abroad.

Euravia dates back to December 1961, a charter airline flying on behalf of tour operators and based at Luton with a fleet of ex-El Al Lockheed Constellations. In the summer of 1964 Euravia was contracted to fly a series of Constellation charters from Rhoose to Barcelona, Palma and Perpignan and a Friday evening highlight was the sight of these four-engine leviathans taxiing to and from Rhoose's relatively small apron alongside Cambrian Dakotas and Viscounts plus Derby Argonauts. With only the 4,534ft of runway 22 available, the fully loaded Euravia Constellations also sent a shudder through the residents of Rhoose village as they launched into the air from the end of runway 22 with no margins for error, just about a positive rate of climb and clawing their way into the air out over the Bristol Channel. Euravia's arrival at Rhoose was a historic event, and the beginning of a lineage of airlines that have served the airport right up to the present. Their first service was on 24 April 1964, when Capt. McDougall flew L-049 Constellation G-AHEN to Palma and Perpignan – another Constellation, G-ARVP, flew services on 15 and 17 May, then G-AHEN again on 26 May and G-ARVP again on 5 June. Euravia had been leasing a Skyways Constellation, G-ARXE, before acquiring it, but retained in its former livery for its first and possibly only visit to Rhoose on the Euravia service on 16 June, arriving from Luton at 0717hrs, flown by a Capt. Chalmers, and then departing to Perpignan at 1117hrs with Capt. Howes in command. This series of Euravia flights from Rhoose ended on 20 October when G-ARVP flew from Palma to Rhoose, before positioning back empty to Luton. In the meantime, on 16 August 1964, having purchased some ex-BOAC Bristol Britannias to replace the Constellations and seeking a more poignant name, the airline became Britannia Airways. In April 1965 Britannia Airways and its owner, Universal Sky Tours, became part of the Thomson travel organisation. Although Britannia Airways didn't operate from Rhoose, that airline's acquisition of Boeing 737-200s in 1968, and the lengthening of Rhoose's runway in 1970, signalled a return for Britannia, flying IT charters to Alicante, Gerona, Ibiza and Palma. In November 1974 Britannia Airways operated a service from Rhoose to Moscow, but throughout the 1970s and 1980s the airline used Boeing 737s and later 757 and 767s for its large programme of IT charters. The year 1982 was also a small landmark for Britannia and many UK regional airports such as Rhoose, when the airline managed to persuade the CAA to allow it to carry a small percentage of seat-only passengers on charter flights. Horizon Travel's airline, Orion Airways, was acquired in August 1988, and Scandinavian holiday operation and airline Blue Scandinavia in 1998, which was trading as TUIfly Nordic Thomson. By 1989 over twenty-six different holiday organisations were offering flights to thirty-three different destinations from Rhoose; ILG and Thomson were the two major operators who were umbrella companies for twenty other smaller package-holiday ones, such as Horizon, Global, Intasun, OSL Apartments, Wings and Skytours. Rhoose was now a very significant charter flight airport.

Britannia and Monarch both benefited from the development of EROPS (Extended Range Operational Performance Standards), which became ETOPS (Extended Range Twin-engine Operational Performance Standards), and allowed their fleets of twin-engine Boeing 757s – and later 767s – to fly across the North Atlantic, previously the domain of only multi-engine 'wide bodies', such as the DC-10 and Boeing 747. Monarch commenced Luton to Orlando flights via a refuelling stop in Gander on 1 May 1988. Similar flights from Rhoose followed in 1989 (see below).

By August 2000 Britannia Airways AB became a wholly owned subsidiary of Preussag (TUI), and the famous Britannia logo on the tail of its aircraft began to disappear. In March 2004 low-fare services were launched under the Thomsonfly brand and on 31 August 2006 the parent company TUI announced a merger of all its constituent European airline compa-

Exeter-based airline British Westpoint operated a a fleet of Dragon Rapides and a Douglas DC-3 in the mid-1960s. At one time in 1964 G-AGSH, the Dragon Rapide pictured, briefly operated schedules. (Geoff Jones)

Euravia – forerunner of Britannia Airways – operated summer charters in 1964. Here is Lockheed Constellation G-AMUP on its 28 August visit. (Geoff Jones)

Skyways Constellation G-ARXE operating a Euravia flight on 16 June 1964, seen at the hold of runway 31 before departure to Perpignan. (Mike Kemp)

In Britannia Airways' initial colours, G-BAZG was a regular at Rhoose from the mid-1970s onwards. (Geoff Jones)

Monarch Airlines Boeing 757-200 G-MONE departs for Florida (Orlando) via a fuel stop in Bangor, Maine – these flights operated from 1989–94. (Malcolm Bradbury)

Globe Air Herald HB-AAH flew a series of winter-time ski charters to Interlaken/Sion in 1966. (Geoff Jones)

A bulb-fields charter to Rotterdam with Lloyd International Britannia G-ANCE in spring 1970. (Kelvin Lumb)

nies under the TUIfly brand. By this time the Britannia Boeing 737, 757 and 767 aircraft seen at Rhoose were flying in the sky-blue colours of TUIfly. The changes were still continuing apace with TUI merging with First Choice in September 2007, and from 1 May 2008 both Thomsonfly and First Choice Airways began operating under a single air operator's certificate, becoming Thomson Airways on 1 May 2009. Through these changes, Thomson have continued to fly from Rhoose; some of their long-haul Boeing 767-300ER flights to Caribbean destinations are extremely popular, but the traditional ones of Alicante, Sharm el-Sheikh, Gran Canaria, Lanzarote, Malaga and Tenerife South provided the majority of the airline's winter 2010/11 schedules at Rhoose. TUI were Rhoose's largest operator in 2010 in terms of passenger numbers.

Never a prolific type at Rhoose, Handley Page's Dart Herald twin turboprop airliner had the rug pulled from under its feet when Cambrian's order for one was cancelled in favour of a deal with BEA and acquisition of Viscount 701s. Nonetheless, a string of Herald users visited Rhoose in the 1960s and later when EAS and Channel Express started cargo and night-time mail flights with them. British Midland's G-ASKK was one of the first on 13 March 1965, followed by Swiss charter airline Globe Air's HB-AAH on 23 February 1966, and then that summer by British United's G-APWG and Autair's G-APWC and 'D in July 1967.

Mention 'bulb charters' and imaginations could run wild with thoughts of air freighters full of electric light bulbs. Not at all! From 1967 and into the 1970s, Welsh tour operators went into frenzied mode each spring flying thousands of passengers on short-break holidays to the Dutch bulb fields, and Rhoose benefited from many of these charters to destinations such as Ostend, Rotterdam and Amsterdam Schiphol. Cambrian operated some, but a melee of other airline operators were recruited to the task – the short-lived Treffield International flew its Viscount in 1967, a rare visit by Bristol Britannias operated by Lloyd International and Donaldson International plus Channel Airways Viscounts and Invicta with Douglas DC-4s.

The air link from Rhoose to Amsterdam has been one of the most enduring features of scheduled passenger services. Dan-Air launched this service in March 1979 in conjunction with KLM, their *Western Mail* advertisement claiming, 'KLM and Dan-Air bring the world closer to Cardiff'. Even back in the 1970s KLM's Schiphol operation was immense with their wide-body fleet of Douglas DC-10s and Boeing 747s operating from here to most major worldwide destinations. This was long before the June 2000 advent of SkyTeam and KLM's close association with Delta Air Lines from the USA. Netherlines, flying Jetstream 31s and Saab 340s, took over from Dan-Air in 1986, flying two daily rotations, and subsequently KLM Cityhopper, a wholly owned subsidiary of KLM Royal Dutch Airlines, took over the service flying Saab 340s, Fokker F50s and currently F70s and F100s, plus the occasional Embraer 190-100. This service has been flown with up to five rotations per day, linking to KLM's main hub at Amsterdam Schiphol Airport. However, 4 April 1994 was a black day for the service when the KLM Cityhopper Saab 340, Flight 433, departed Schiphol for Rhoose but had to return to Schiphol with a problem. During an attempted 'go-around', the aircraft crashed and of the twenty-four on board three were killed, including the captain, and nine on board received serious injuries.

Air France preceded the arrival of KLM at Rhoose, and amidst great excitement at welcoming the first major European airline to operate schedules, introduced weekday services between Paris Charles de Gaulle and Rhoose, the first service flown on 26 March 1990 using a thirty-three-seat Saab 340 belonging to Air France franchisee, BritAir. In October 1991, due to the popularity of the afternoon service, a larger forty-six-seat ATR-42 was introduced. This service, like those to Amsterdam, was sold heavily on the basis of passenger inter-lining for onward Air France connections worldwide. Air France ceased this service when Manx Airlines – which started operating the route in October 1991 – started up in competition and then took over completely.

Lengthening of the runway at Rhoose to 7,000ft in 1970 was always promoted as the opportunity for the airport to handle direct transatlantic flights. The very first commercial transatlantic

Opposite from top

Netherlands Airlines for European Commuter Services was the full name, or just NetherLines for short. This airline took over the Amsterdam schedules from Dan-Air in 1986 –Jetstream 31 PH-KJF awaits its passengers on 26 November 1986. (Geoff Jones)

KLM Cityhopper Saab 340 PH-KSL prepares for departure to Amsterdam in August 1993. (Geoff Jones)

Fokker 50 turboprops were replaced by Fokker 100 and Fokker 70 jets, the latter still the main-stay of the Amsterdam schedules in 2011. PH-KZA, an F70, is pictured in January 2005. (Geoff Jones)

flight to make full use of this new asset was on 7 October 1971, when for £8,700 (return) ninety members of the Pendyrus Male Choir chartered British Caledonian Airways Boeing 707-399C G-AVKA for a flight to San Francisco – as well as the choir, composer Dr Alan Hoddinott (then Professor of Music at University College, Cardiff) and Aeronwy Thomas (daughter of Dylan Thomas) were on board, the latter to recite poems during the US tour. This was a big event in the history of South Wales aviation, the choir receiving an official message from the Secretary of State for Wales, Rt Hon. Peter Thomas QC MP, to speed them on their way. The aircraft captained by A.R. Warren positioned in from London Gatwick and then as Charter Flight Number CA1469 routed out to San Francisco (Oakland) via Keflavik for a fuel stop – the return flight was flown on 24 October by G-AVTW, which arrived at Rhoose from New York at 2118hrs and then positioned back to London Gatwick at 0017hrs. John H. Lewis, still the choir's general secretary, signed the Aircraft Charter Agreement with Caledonian Airways back in 1971, organised through Bethel Gwyn & Co. Ltd, Newport travel agents, and remembers several hours' delay to the flight's departure due to unprecedented fog at Rhoose which delayed the arrival of the 707 from London Gatwick. The ninety members of the choir were not perturbed and in the small, now crowded, old terminal on the airport's south side, gathered for some impromptu choral practice, with conductor Glynne Jones heading up the unscheduled entertainment for check-in and other airport staff. On the flight to Iceland at 21,000ft choir member Carl Bowen remembers the 'sea of cloud down below and at quarter to six we spot the rugged and barren coast of Iceland – we were served drinks by our delightful stewardesses who experienced some difficulties with *Don Juan* choristers'. After San Francisco, the tour took the choir to Sacramento, Vancouver, Calgary, Chicago, Wyoming, Toronto, London (Ontario) and Youngstown (Ohio) before hitting the Big Apple and their return flight to Rhoose.

This historic charter was followed in November by a rare visit on a military trooping charter to Gütersloh, West Germany, of a Vickers VC-10. G-ATDJ was one of the four long-range, T-tail, four-engine transports in the fleet of British United Airways (BUA), and normally based at London Gatwick. Caledonian Airways had just taken over BUA, including all of its fleet of thirty-one aircraft, and at the time of its Rhoose visit the VC-10 was in the rarely seen livery of Caledonian/BUA. It was parked on the new concrete apron to the north of the Cambrian hangar, before the airport's new terminal was opened, and after some tight ground manoeuvres made a departure from runway 12.

It was tour operator Jetsave that took the next major initiative and, in conjunction with Canadian airline CP Air (inaugurated as Canadian Pacific Airlines in January 1942), with Douglas DC-8-43 flights to Toronto starting on 1 July 1977. Occasionally CP Air substituted an Air Canada DC-8 for their own, as on 8 and 12 June 1978. CP Air was a regular feature of the summer scene at Rhoose and introduced their 'stretched' DC-8, the DC-8-63, in 1980 on the weekly service to Toronto. Their Boeing 747-200 replaced the DC-8s in 1981, a momentous occasion for the airport with the first CF-CRD arriving on 2 June, followed by one of the airline's Douglas DC-10s C-GCPE on 1 September. CP Air continued operations until at least 1983. Wardair, Nationair, Worldways and Air Transat were other Canadian airlines that used Rhoose, using respectively Boeing 747s, Nationair with DC-8-63s and the latter Boeing 757s and Airbus A310s.

Pendyrus Male Choir's conductor Glynne Jones (beard and cravat) gets in the limelight on the forecourt of the terminal building before the choir's October 1971 departure to the USA. (Via Carl Bowen)

There was a party atmosphere on the apron prior to the Pendyrus Male Choir boarding their chartered Boeing 707 for the flight from Rhoose to San Francisco in October 1971. (Carl Bowen)

The 'bat man' working hard to guide this Caledonian/BUA Vickers VC-10 from the 'play-pen' parking on its way to Gütersloh in West Germany in 1971. (Kelvin Lumb)

CP Air Douglas DC-10-30 C-GCPH on turn-around on 1 September 1981. (Kelvin Lumb)

Engulfed by support vehicles, Wardair's Boeing 747-1D1 C-FDJC, one of only two the airline operated at the time, at turn-around on arrival from Toronto in May 1988. (Geoff Jones)

In April 1981, Air Florida's Douglas DC-10-30 departs runway 12 for Orlando (via Belfast) at the start of the season of transatlantic services. (Geoff Jones)

The inaugural American Trans Air flight to New York (JFK) on 9 July 1996; Boeing 757 N754AT. (Malcolm Bradbury)

A landmark year for Rhoose was 1981, with several other transatlantic flights and services. Air Florida's debut was significant, with their wide-body tri-jet Douglas DC-10 and the start of weekly flights to Florida, which had become the vacation destination of choice thanks to Mickey Mouse and his friends. The first flight from Rhoose was on 23 April 1981, when DC-10-30CF N1035F was chartered by 4 Seasons Travel Centre of Pontypridd to fly 288 passengers to Miami via a fuel stop in Prestwick, Scotland. The return flight was flown direct. Continuing the 1981 transatlantic theme was the 31 July charter of World Airways Douglas DC-8-63CF N806WA for a flight to Des Moines, Iowa, via Shannon. Again the return was direct. Subsequently transatlantic flights to Orlando were flown fortnightly by Monarch on behalf of the International Leisure Group starting on 4 May 1989 (G-BNSE) and routing via Bangor, Maine, using Boeing 757s – they also flew to Orlando in 1990 and through to 1994, by which time the service had become weekly. Britannia also flew to Orlando starting in 1993, using their Boeing 767s which were able to operate direct using Sanford up to 1996 and then the main Orlando International Airport (MCO). Air Europe operated several 757 flights from Rhoose to Bangor, Maine, in May and August 1990, presumably also continuing on to the Orlando area. Canadian flights from Rhoose became a permanent feature of the airport for many years, subsequently with Wardair in 1988 with Boeing 747-100s, Worldways with DC-8-63s and in 1995 Air Transat using Boeing 757s. In 2007 Rhoose again had transatlantic services to Canada on its schedules, this time with Ottawa-based Zoom Airlines using their Boeing 767-300ERs, but on 28 August 2008 the airline ceased operations and Rhoose was again without a direct Canadian link. Starting in 1989 on Fridays from 16 June ATA (American Trans Air) operated a direct New York JFK to Rhoose service using Boeing 757s, but which routed back to New York via London Gatwick – the following year from June they did the same but returned to JFK via Birmingham, and on a few occasions the service was flown by one of their Lockheed L1011 Tristars. These flights were operated by Globespan and American Airplan. This was not the first time an ATA aircraft had visited Rhoose – in summer 1987 Air Malta leased ATA's Boeing 727-51 N287AT, which made several visits. Discussions about a direct transatlantic link surfaced again in 2010 with US airline Delta Air Lines who have been developing their international hub at New York's JFK Airport – unfortunately the talks came to nought.

Eastern promise was much in evidence at Rhoose in the 1970s and 1980s, the East being Eastern Europe, all adding to the cosmopolitan feel at the airport. Ilyushin IL-18s had visited in 1980 and in the pre-*glasnost* days prior to 1988, the sight of an Aeroflot Tupolev jet airliner on the apron at Rhoose was a 'pinch yourself' moment. However, on 17 October 1981 Tu-134A CCCP-65769 arrived at Rhoose, positioning in from Glasgow, chartered by Hourmont Holidays to take a group of tourists to Moscow. The return Tu-134 flight arrived back at Rhoose from Leningrad a week later. The Welsh National Youth Orchestra flew to Dresden on 12 April 1980 using the Polish national airline LOT and their Ilyushin IL-18D SP-LSI and in June the East German airline Interflug operated no fewer than four IL-18 charter flights to transport the Welsh National Opera to East Berlin. On 1 June DM-STO arrived

During winter 1999 Austrian airline Tyrolean flew Saturday skiing charters to Innsbruck with their Fokker F70s; OE-LFJ pictured here on 2 January 1999. (Geoff Jones)

followed by 'TB the next day. For the return on 15 June both DM-STH and 'TB arrived, but one had departed before the other arrived. Charter flights to Adriatic resorts were also popular, this pre-Balkan Wars and the division of the former Yugoslavia, with Split a popular destination. In 1980 a series of JAT (Jugoslovenski Aerotransport) charters using Douglas DC-9-32s were operated from Rhoose and later in the decade supplemented by Aviogenex with their Tupolev Tu-134s and Boeing 727. Tri-jet Tupolev Tu-154s were also regulars at Rhoose from the 1980s up until 2002, first those of state-owned Balkan Bulgarian Airlines, followed from 1999 by the privatised Balkan until that airline was declared bankrupt in March 2001 and government-owned Balkan Air Tours (Balkan Holidays) took over in December 2002; all of these operators were flying from Rhoose to the Black Sea resorts of Varna and Bourgas.

Not only airlines contributed to the burgeoning holiday travel flights at Rhoose. If it weren't for the tour operators and travel agent – this before the days of independent internet booking – then the growth of Rhoose would have been much less dramatic. In 1994 new tour opera-tors introduced a range of new services to Rhoose, these including Avro, Unijet, Inspirations and Saga. Avro traded on the strap line 'The UK's Number One Flight Only Operator', a by-product of Britannia's 1982 permission from the CAA. Avro celebrated their arrival in style, giving away flights in a prize draw. In the heat of July 1998 television weather presenter Siân Lloyd arrived at Rhoose complete with unseasonable winter ski gear. She was involved in a promotion on behalf of Skier's World, together with the airport's sales and marketing director, Caroline Godfrey, to promote the upcoming winter sports destinations available from Rhoose. Innsbruck, Austria, with Tyrolean Airways Fokker 70s was one of these during winter 1998/99. The Rhoose regulars such as Thomson/TUI also served several popular ski destinations and, for a short while, bmibaby schedules from Rhoose to Munich and Geneva served skiers want-ing to reach the nearby slopes of the Austrian Tyrol and western Alps.

Capital Airlines, which was founded in 1983 at Leeds/Bradford Airport as Brown Air, took advantage of the failure of Dan-Air subsidiary Metropolitan Airways and commenced sched-ules on the Rhoose–Glasgow route in August 1985, flying via the airline's home at Leeds/ Bradford initially using a Short SD3-30 in April 1987, but then a larger Short SD3-60. A direct service to Glasgow was inaugurated and, from summer 1988, a service to Jersey in the Channel Islands. However, Capital went the way of many UK regional airlines and on 28 June 1990 all operations by the airline were suspended because of financial problems of the parent company.

Eastern Airlines commenced schedules at Rhoose on 24 April 2006 using Jetstream 41s, some of which had been based at Rhoose during the Manx Airlines era – the service linked Rhoose with Aberdeen, Newcastle and Brussels. This was as a direct result of Air Wales' withdrawal of all their scheduled services. Eastern Airlines started operations in December 1997 and in February 1999 purchased Manchester-based Air Kilroe, a former Rhoose operator, who in 1993 operated a twice-daily scheduled Jetstream 31 service to and from Manchester.

An exciting new development on 30 March 2011 was the commencement of direct, four times a week schedules from Rhoose to Zurich by Helvetic Airways, using their Fokker 100 jets. Helvetic (initially known as Odette Airways until September 2003) are Zurich-based and have been operating low-fare flights from Zurich to several European destinations since February 2002. This is the first direct non-ski schedule from Rhoose to a Swiss city.

Diversions

Rhoose has always sold itself as 'a fair-weather airport' or 'the all-weather operations airport', happy to take diversions from the UK's major airports when their weather deteriorates. Writing in the 1992 Airport Handbook, managing director Graham Greaves described Rhoose as 'enjoying an all year round good weather record, and over the last twenty-five years, the meteorological conditions have been second only to Prestwick (in Scotland) throughout the UK'. By this time both Virgin Atlantic and Pan American Airways had designated Rhoose as their first alternate diversionary airport. There have been many days when passenger misery at news of a diversion has been contrasted with the airport authority's pleasure at being able to welcome airliners large and small. The first documented was a Derby Airways Miles Marathon from Jersey on 9 August 1959 at 2153hrs because its intended stop at Bournemouth for customs couldn't take place as that airport had closed for the night.

Weather at the hill-top Bristol Lulsgate Airport has often been an issue, and Rhoose has been – and still is – a welcome bolt hole for easyJet and other airline traffic unable to land there. On 6 January 2007, whilst Bristol was experiencing difficulties regarding its runway surface and an Aurigny Air Services ATR-72 slid off the runway on to the grass, some flights diverted to Rhoose and with five easyJet Airbus aircraft on the western apron you had to pinch yourself that you weren't at Bristol. On 30 November 1975, Rhoose experienced its first really big 'diversion day' following the opening of the lengthened runway – both London Heathrow and Gatwick airports were closed due to fog – when Rhoose welcomed an assortment of diverting British Airways aircraft from Heathrow, a trio of Tridents, G-AWZX inbound from Rome, G-AYEX from Tripoli and one from Helsinki, plus a BAC1-11 from Berlin. Diverting from Gatwick were two British Caledonian aircraft, a BAC1-11 from Alicante and a Boeing 707 G-AYEX from Tenerife. Other notable London Gatwick diversions occurred on 13 June 1977 when Laker Airways DC-10 G-BELO diverted to Rhoose, followed early on the morning of 21 January 1979 by the same Laker 'Skytrain' Douglas DC-10 on its eastbound sector from New York, when the Sussex airport was fog-bound and the captain elected to divert to Rhoose.

During the 1980s, the German government began preparing Lufthansa for privatisation – the airline was mired in labour disputes and strikes. Rhoose was the chosen diversion airport, several Airbus A300s destined for German airports making landfall in South Wales. Several of the airline's Boeing 737s also landed at Rhoose.

There have been several 'monumental diversion days' at Rhoose. One remembered by air traffic control and ground-handling staff alike was on 26 November 1993, when nine 'heavies', eight Boeing 747s and a DC-10, could not land at Gatwick and Heathrow, diverting to Rhoose.

These included Continental (Flight 04 from Houston), United Airlines (Flight 930 from San Francisco), British Airways and Virgin Atlantic Boeing 747s – one of Virgin's 747s (G-TKYO) had departed Tokyo at 0318hrs GMT and arrived at Rhoose at 1555hrs GMT. Later a Virgin Airbus A340 was a notable first, and soon after a Virgin Atlantic 747 also diverted, landed safely, but then managed to slide off the icy taxiway right in front of the control tower. Other Virgin Atlantic diversions have touched down at Rhoose over the years for an assortment of reasons; in August 1996 Boeing 747-400 G-VBIG was one of these, before departing to Heathrow later in the day.

During the unseasonable snows of late November and December 2010 London Gatwick Airport was closed for nearly three days at the beginning of December. Rhoose welcomed Gatwick-bound Thomson Boeing 757s from Arrecife on 30 November, the next day a Monarch Airbus A321 from Paphos, a Thomson 737 diverted from Edinburgh and a CityJet RJ85 from London City. The snows continued and even Rhoose was closed for a while on Saturday and Sunday 18 and 19 December, but on the 18th welcomed both Monarch and Thomson Boeings and Airbus aircraft which couldn't land at Stansted, Luton and Gatwick, all closed because of snow.

Cargo Operations

These could occupy a whole book, such is the diversity of the operations – the amazing variability of freight tonnages is also notable (see Appendix 2). One of the most significant stimuli to freight totals was the 1980 opening of the large Ford engine plant at Bridgend. Even before this Ford had factories in South Wales (Jersey Marine, Swansea), a compact alternator plant at Miskin plus many sub-contractors, with visits to these generating corporate traffic and air-freight charters. A notable example of this was in August 1979 with the arrival of the Irish airline Aer Turas and their all-cargo Canadair CL-44J EI-BGO with its swing-tail cargo access. Post-1980 the air freighting of parts and components between the Bridgend Ford plant and those in Germany, Belgium and Spain has seen innumerable cargo charters, including HeavyLift Belfast G-BEPS and Air Omega using their Embraer EMB120 Brasilias.

Treffield Aviation, formed at Sywell Aerodrome in September 1965, operated two Avro Ansons on miscellaneous freight charters. They planned to operate scheduled freight services from Rhoose and had already approached the airport committee in May 1965 to seek exemption from landing fees for their first six months of operations at Rhoose, a request that was granted.

However, one of the first big 'cargo events' at Rhoose was on the evening of Monday 26 August 1968 when the Penarth Road Cardiff-based engineering company Powell-Duffryn chartered an Invicta Airlines Douglas DC-4 G-ASEN. They had to transport 5 tons of air-conditioning equipment to their customer in Switzerland, so with this delivered to Rhoose's apron by a convoy of lorries, it was loaded manually into the rear cargo door of the 1944 vintage, ex-USAAF DC-4 for carriage to Basle, Switzerland. This ex-military C-54, now a DC-4, had flown with Pan American, Canadian Pacific, Icelandair, Starways and Ace freighters before joining Manston, Kent-based Invicta in April 1966, staying with the airline until exported to South Africa in February 1971.

By 1978 Rhoose was being advertised as 'Cargo Centre for Wales', the airport's 15,000 sq. ft cargo building the focus for international import and exports. Customs granted the airport the facility for inter-port removal of containers and surface vehicles from all destinations. Very little of the total freight volume was actually arriving or leaving by air, but Rhoose became a recognised cargo distribution centre '... which will develop further with the completion of the envisaged Newport to Swansea M4 link in conjunction with an access road to the airport from the new motorway'. As we all know this access road link has still not happened twenty-five years later. Another air cargo initiative in the 1970s was the establishment by Chenshire Ltd of an airport office in 1974 from which livestock exports by air were co-ordinated. In 1977 over

With fog at Heathrow and Gatwick, Rhoose handled several diversions on 30 November 1975, including a BCAL Boeing 707 and British Airways Trident III (Cardiff Airport)

26 November 1993 was a major 'diversion day', with nine wide-body diversions including Continental 04 from Houston to Gatwick and United 930 from San Francisco to Gatwick. Also on this day, VIR 901 G-TKYO arrived at 15.55 from Tokyo Narita. (Malcolm Bradbury)

Beautiful study of a Laker Skytrain DC-10, G-FGAL 'Northern Belle', diverted from Gatwick in 1980. (Kelvin Lumb)

N707ME Arrow Air Boeing 707. (Mike Freshney Collection)

Air New Zealand Boeing 747-400 ZK-NBT on arrival at Rhoose on 25 September 1996 direct from Auckland. (Barry Webb via Cardiff Airport)

HeavyLift Shorts Belfast freighter G-BEPS being loaded with Ford engine components during 1993. This aircraft visited again, with St Athan closed, arriving from Ascension carrying Tornado F3 ZG753 which had 'gone tech' there. (Kelvin Lumb)

HeavyLift Il-76 RA-76758 transporting Ford engine components from their Bridgend plant to Spain via Rhoose on 23 March 1993. (Malcolm Bradbury)

6,000 head of cattle were flown out from Rhoose to France, Belgium, Italy and Saudi Arabia.

In 1979 the Royal Mail established its Skynet week-night airmail network with Liverpool Airport as its hub for this service, which they called Datapost, a courier-style next-day operation for urgent packages and computer data. During the winter of 1979/80 two Piper Aztecs from Biggin Hill-based Euroair kicked off this nightly Rhoose to Liverpool service, before introduction of a single BN-2 Islander. In 1980 Executive Express, whose main base was at Luton, started a similar Rhoose–Luton–Rhoose night-mail run using Cessna 404 Titan aircraft, including G-MSDS. Well-known Rhoose-based pilot Capt. Cliff Hubbard flew this for a while after he retired from British Airways. Another company called Euroflite also did the Datapost run for a while in 1982 with Cessna 404 Titans, including the appropriately registered G-RUSH. Manchester-based Telair flew mail services to Liverpool for a while in 1983 in conjunction with its south–north BN-2 Islander passenger service, but was replaced by Bournemouth-based Channel Express, whose DHC-6 Twin Otter G-RBLA flew nightly between Bournemouth and Liverpool with intermediate stops at Bristol and Rhoose. Channel Express, formed from Express Air Services (EAS) under the chairmanship of Philip Meeson, became a regular sight at Rhoose later in the 1980s and 1990s, when one of their fleet of HPR.7 Herald freighters was based there. After this Channel Express Lockheed L188 Electra freighters were also regulars at Rhoose, plus in 1996 their Fokker F27 freighters, one of them G-CEXB regaled in a special 'Parcel Force' livery. Philip Meeson went on to found the low-fare passenger airline Jet2 and their Boeing 737s have visited Rhoose on ad hoc charters on many occasions.

In 1984 another new player arrived on the air freight scene at Rhoose, Jersey European Airways (JEA), forerunner of today's flybe. One of their Twin Otters (G-OJEA or G-BKBC) flew the nightly mail flight to Liverpool, but during the weekdays all the seats were reinstalled and it flew a morning and evening scheduled passenger service from Rhoose via Bristol to London Gatwick and back. JEA had an inter-line agreement with British Caledonian at Gatwick so many of the passengers were continuing via Gatwick to destinations on BCal's worldwide network – this was in the pre-M25 era so the flying from Rhoose to Gatwick did save considerable time against the long drive. On the weekends during the summer of 1985 JEA's Twin Otter flew from Rhoose to the Isle of Man via Bristol and back, but by 1986 the M25 had been opened and the passenger numbers on the Gatwick service dwindled and JEA pulled out of both freight and passenger operations at Rhoose. Hubbardair replaced them on the night-mail flights to Liverpool, again with a Twin Otter, but only survived a couple of months.

Other operators continued to come and go. In 1986–87 DC-3s returned to regular operations at Rhoose after a gap of twenty years, when Coventry-based Air Atlantique used a DC-3 for the nightly Liverpool service, plus ad hoc charter work – this was frequently supplemented by one of the airline's DC-6s, mainly for car parts charters. Biggin Hill-based Fairflight also got involved in night-time mail and air freight at Rhoose around this time using a Short SD-330, followed by another SD-330 operator Southend-based National Airways, who also used Bandeirantes. Celtic Airways arrived around 1990, operating their Short SD-330s and later Dutch-registered Fokker F27s up until about 1995, when the airline ceased operations. About 1992 the Royal Mail's Skynet hub was moved from Liverpool to East Midlands Airport (EMA) at Castle Donington, so all night-time mail flights from Rhoose now headed north-east to EMA. Newcastle-based Gill Air got in on the act for a while in the 1990s, with aircraft from their large fleet of Short SD-330s, then Liverpool-based Emerald Airways and Reed Aviation in 1997–98 with one of their various HS.748 turboprop twins, until the arrival of BAC Express (formerly BAC Aircraft, established in 1992) and their Short SD-360s, who as well as having the contract with Royal Mail/Consignia also flew for FedEx and other express courier companies throughout Europe. The Royal Mail flights from Rhoose ceased around 2004 and after this the mail went by road from South Wales to Bristol, from where they were flown to EMA. However, with the 2010 closure of the Bristol Royal Mail facility there are, at the time of writing, rumours that a Bournemouth-based aircraft of Atlantic Airlines may fly the mail for South

Opposite from top

Manston, Kent-based Invicta Airlines Douglas DC-4 G-ASEN was chartered by Powell-Duffryn to export air conditioning equipment to Basle in August 1965. (Cardiff Airport)

With the award of the overnight mail contract and several other charter contracts, Celtic Airways grew rapidly in 1989–90, first with Shorts SD3-30s (G-BHHU and 'IYH), then with larger Fokker F.27s. (Geoff Jones)

EAS Cargo Boeing 707 5N-ASY, although registered in Nigeria, was operated on cargo charters from Ostend and visited in 1992. (Kelvin Lumb)

Wales from the EMA hub to Rhoose, before positioning back empty to Bournemouth.

Arrival at Rhoose of an Aeronaves del Peru Douglas DC-8-54F (OB-1300) on 4 July 1990 was a huge surprise, apparently shipping livestock to South America. The 1990s was the era of 'classic' four-engine freighters, converted ex-passenger DC-8s and 707s – a really unusual one visited Rhoose in January 1992, a Boeing 707-323C in the colours of Air Gambia but registered EL-AKC, a Liberian identity, complemented around the same time by another Boeing 707-351C Nigerian registered (5N-ASY) but based at Ostend, Belgium, with EAS Cargo Airlines. An equally exotic cargo visitor arrived on 27 May 1994, the Ugandan registered Boeing 707-379C of Dairo Air Service (DAS) 5X-JEF, chartered by Oxfam to transport jeeps and relief supplies to Rwanda – it departed Rhoose as the DSR414 for Rotterdam and then Athens before heading south to its destination in Africa; sister ship 5X-JET visited in August.

HeavyLift Short Belfast G-BEPS has visited on several occasions including in February 1991 and on 20 July 1997 whilst shipping the fuselage of an RAF Tornado F3 jet (ZG753) back to St Athan (which was closed) from Ascension, where it had 'gone tech' whilst flying from the Falklands. A Volga Dnepr Antonov An-124-100 (RA-82074) did a similar flight on 27 January 2000, returning two Tornado F3s from the Falklands (ZG774 and '776) to DARA at St Athan, flying in via Ascension and departing Rhoose to Ulyanovsk Vostochny in Russia (which incidentally has the third-longest public-use runway in the world at 16,405ft). The first Boeing C-17 Globemaster freighter aircraft, a huge monster of an aircraft capable of carrying 169,000lb of cargo, and at this time one of the first leased by the Royal Air Force, made its debut at Rhoose in 2001. Seven of the UK's top freight forwarding companies have branch offices and warehouse space at Rhoose, including DFDS Transport (UK), Air Cargo Wales, BAX Global, Servisair Cargo, Eagle Global Logistics, Nippon Express and Raven Express.

More recently in 2005 and 2006, the Liege Belgium-based air freight specialist TNT Airways operated regular express freight flights from Rhoose using BAe146s and occasionally their Boeing 737-300s. In 2003 Atlantic Air Lines (an associate of Channel Express) brought further diversity to Rhoose's air cargo scene by operating a series of flights with its unusual high-wing twin jet, the Antonov An-74-200 (UR74057) leased from Latvian airline RAF-Avia.

7

SPORTING AND OTHER AIRLIFTS AND DISPLAYS

After the tragedy at RAF Llandow on 12 March 1950 when a Fairflight Avro Tudor G-AKBY crashed, the opening of Rhoose and its use for the annual migrations of Welsh rugby supporters was inevitable. At the time this Llandow crash was 'the world's worst air disaster', when just three of eighty-three occupants on the Tudor survived the landing accident when the aircraft was returning from Belfast with rugby supporters. However, even up until the late 1960s, when the runway was extended at Rhoose, some of the subsequent airlift aircraft and those on other special charters with larger aircraft that couldn't safely land on Rhoose's 3,700ft or 4,534ft runways continued to use RAF St Athan with its longer, 6,000ft runway.

The Ireland *v.* Wales rugby international in Dublin on 10 March 1956 was one of the first large airlifts to operate from Rhoose, primarily with Aer Lingus (see Chapter 2) providing most of the capacity to carry Welsh supporters across the Irish Sea to Dublin. A total of twenty-five extra Aer Lingus flights were scheduled, with their DC-3s carrying nearly 1,000 supporters, and Friday 9 March saw ten extra flights. The busiest day for Aer Lingus was Sunday 11 March, when twenty-four extra flights were scheduled between Dublin and Rhoose bringing the Welsh supporters home after an 11-3 defeat by the Irishmen.

The 1959 airlift for the France *v.* Wales rugby international in Paris was a fairly low-key affair with a rejuvenated Cambrian Airways flying ten round trips with Welsh supporters between Rhoose and Paris (Le Bourget) using three of its DC-3s or Pionairs (the name coined by the state airline BEA for the DC-3), G-AHCZ, G-AMFV and G-AMJX on 2 and 3 April. An Eagle Airways Vickers Viking G-AHPM was chartered to provide extra capacity and flew one service to Le Bourget on 3 April.

For the 1960 Five Nations season Wales played Ireland at Lansdowne Road in Dublin and France were in Cardiff. So on 10 March Aer Lingus launched a huge operation to carry Welsh supporters to Dublin using no less than six of their Viscounts (EI-AJI, 'JJ, 'JK, 'KK, 'KL and 'KC), which made a total of fifteen round trips between Rhoose and Dublin. On the following day Cambrian and Derby Airways joined in with a further twenty-one round trips with Pionairs and DC-3s, the two Derby ones being G-AOGZ and G-APBC. Further flights to Dublin were made by Dan-Air DC-3 G-AMSU on 11 March. For the return east to Rhoose across the Irish Sea, Eagle Airways Viking G-AHPM was used again on 13 March, providing some air transport variety and carrying some of the jubilant Welsh supporters who had seen their team defeat the Irish 10–9. It appears that Aer Lingus was not involved in the flights to return Welsh supporters to Rhoose – perhaps smarting from the Irish defeat – with other flights flown by three BKS Air Transport DC-3s, G-AMSH, G-AMVC and G-APPO. No fewer than ten DC-3s were busy shuttling supporters between Dublin and Rhoose, from Cambrian, Dan-Air, Derby and BKS.

For the French rugby team's visit to Cardiff for the rugby international on 26 March 1960, the Air France Lockheed L-749A Constellation F-BAZO arrived at Rhoose from Paris Orly late on the Thursday afternoon with the team, officials and supporters – this aircraft then departed empty back to France. On the morning of the match the tempo and variety increased at Rhoose with the arrival of Tradair Viking G-APOR, Independent Viking G-AJCE, Silver City DC-3 G-ANLF, UAT Nord 2502 Noratlas F-BGZG (from Le Bourget) and, finally at midday arriving from Paris Orly, just a couple of hours before the kick-off, TAI Douglas C-54A Skymaster F-BDRJ. The return flights were operated with the same aircraft, with the exception of Air France L-749A Constellation F-BAZP, which returned to Paris Orly on 27 March with the victorious French team.

The French rugby airlift on 21 March 1962 was epic, if only for the fact that one of the air-craft that arrived at Rhoose – from Paris Le Bourget – was the Boeing Model 307 Stratoliner F-BELY, one of five acquired in 1951 by the French airline Aigle Azur, three of which were then seconded to south-east Asia to fly between Saigon and Hanoi. The aircraft to land at Rhoose was in the colours of Air Laos, but was one of two Stratoliners in the fleet operated by the Nice-based charter and IT operator Airnautic (Air France took a majority shareholding in Airnautic early in 1962). Only ten examples of the Stratoliner, this iconic pre-war airliner, were ever built and the prototype had first flown on 31 December 1938, destined for Pan American Airways. One of the type was acquired by Howard Hughes in 1938 for an attempt on his own round-the-world flight record, but the outbreak of the Second World War meant the cancel-lation of this plan, and Hughes had the aircraft converted to an ultra-deluxe personal aircraft. The Stratoliner was essentially a Boeing B-17C fitted with a roomy, pressurised, passenger-type fuselage. The 1962 airlift was also the first chance for observers at Rhoose to see an airliner in the colours of the French domestic airline Air Inter, Douglas DC-4 F-BDRJ. Air Inter aircraft were rarely seen outside the borders of France, having been formed in November 1954 and initially operating charter flights, but from March 1958 onwards a series of domestic schedules were brought in using DC-3s and DC-4s. Other 1962 French visitors included two Air France DC-4s F-BBDR and F-BHBX plus the same airline's DC-3 F-BFGV. However, to round off a stunning airlift, the largest aircraft ever to land at Rhoose arrived from Paris on 25 March in the shape of Air France Lockheed L-1049G Super Constellation F-BHBJ.

During the March 1966 French rugby airlift RAF St Athan was the favoured destination for Air France and their Lockheed L1049 Constellation F-BHBE, whilst another Constellation, DC-3s, the European Aero Services Vickers Viking F-OCEU and a multitude of lighter air-craft used Rhoose. Another charter that had to use RAF St Athan rather than Rhoose was on 18 April 1966 when the National Youth Orchestra of Wales embarked on a tour of Germany. The German charter airline Südflug (*Süddeutsche Fluggesellschaft*), based in Stuttgart, was con-tracted for the airlift of musicians and their instruments using the Douglas DC-7C D-ABAD, one of six in their fleet. D-ABAC was used for the return charter on 25 April.

The airlifts continued through the 1960s, 1970s and to the present day, even-numbered years the French were away from home in Cardiff and odd-numbered the Irish. The biennial French airlifts to Rhoose continued to be a highlight, the bonhomie of the often well-oiled supporters complemented by a range of unusual and interesting aircraft chartered. The 1970 airlift was the last graced by the exotic lines of the Lockheed Constellations, the world's civil airliner fleets having largely turned to turboprops or jets – no worries about short runways or using St Athan: Rhoose's new runway was now open for business and 7,000ft in length. 4 April 1970 was a classic day at Rhoose in the shadow of the newly commissioned control tower on the airport's north-east boundary, with three Lockheed L-1049G Super Constellations of charter airline Catair (F-BGNG, 'HMI and 'RAD) and two Douglas DC-6A of Trans Union (F-BNUZ and 'RID) arriving. Once the passengers had been disembarked to the terminal, the aircraft parking problem was solved with the aircraft taxiing to the 'old runway' 12/22 for parking. Donaldson

Air France Douglas DC-4 F-BILL manoeuvres on the main apron at Rhoose on 26 March 1966 on arrival from Paris. (Geoff Jones)

Amongst a large tranche of interesting aircraft that characterised the March 1970 French rugby airlift was this Trans Union Douglas DC-6B, F-BRID. (Kelvin Lumb)

For the 1972 French rugby airlift a group of supporters chartered this Beech C-45G F-BHMM to fly from Le Bourget. That year, all French visiting aircraft were parked on the 12/22 cross runway for the first time. (Geoff Jones)

Catair Constellation F-BGNG dwarfs some enthusiasts in the public enclosure during the April 1970 French rugby airlift – at the time, just a white wooden fence separated public from the air-side operations. (Tony Merton-Jones)

and Britannia Airways Britannias flew in (G-APNB and G-ANBO respectively), the rare sight of an Air Inter Viscount (F-BGNO) as they usually only operated French domestic services, an EAS Herald F-BOIZ, BMA Viscount G-AVJB and a South West Aviation Dakota G-APBC. What a weekend for the air spotters and photographers!

The 1972 airlift around Saturday 25 March saw the first use of jets, and being French they were Caravelles, F-BJTF (Air Charter International), F-BSEL and F-BTDL (Euralair). A trio of Armée de l'Air MS.760 Paris jets breezed in and a Hawker Siddeley HS.125 executive jet F-BPMC belonging to champagne company Moet et Chandon. The last DC-6B to be seen on an airlift graced the Rhoose tarmac, Europe Aero Service's ex-Sabena F-BOEV, an evocative Beech 18 twin (F-BHMM) and a Rousseau Aviation HS.748 turboprop. Runway 12/22 was used for parking, as it has been for all subsequent larger events right up to the 2010 Ryder Cup.

As the transports used for subsequent airlifts evolved, aircraft big and small flew in, the EAS Vanguards, the ACI Boeing 727s, more Caravelles, Fokker F28s, F27s, Beechcraft 99s, Heralds, BN Islanders, Airbuses and, in 1994 and 1996, AOM DC-10s. When Wales travelled overseas to Dublin, Rhoose also became extremely busy – one such year was 1996 when the team departed on 29 February on a chartered Britannia Boeing 767. There were also four Swedish-registered Air Ops Lockheed L1011 Tristars used, plus another Tristar G-BBAI of Caledonian Airways using an Aer Lingus call-sign, two Aer Lingus Boeing 737s, another Britannia 767 and a Translift Airbus A300 (EI-CJK). The match on 2 March was a win for Ireland 30:17, despite a try from Ieuan Evans. The thousands of supporters, well 'oiled' after a night of drowning their sorrows in Dublin, arrived back at Rhoose in their fleet of chartered aircraft the following day. And in 1999, when the Rugby World Cup came to Wales, Rhoose Airport had never seen anything like it, the final on 6 November seeing a huge influx of aircraft and over fifty executive jets, the runway 12/22 parking almost full to bursting and the apron in front of the BAMC hangar also utilised.

By 2010 the French rugby team and officials enjoyed the luxury of an Air France Boeing 777 for their short flight from Paris to Rhoose. Blue Line, now resigned to memory, operated plenty of charters in 2010 with their Fokker 100, MD-83 and Airbus A310, and Europe Airpost provided no fewer than six Boeing 737-300s. A total of 6,500 fans and officials were airlifted to Rhoose to see their team beat Wales. Plenty of smaller types were also chartered, including the Régional Embraer 135ER F-GRGP from Lyon St Exupery and two Spanish-registered Swearingen SA-227 Metro IIIs of Aeronova. Whilst the Welsh fans travelling abroad usually charter an assortment of aircraft to fly from Rhoose to Paris, Dublin and Edinburgh, providing heightened activity at the airport, as well as in the Scrum-Half terminal bar, the French airlift inbound to Rhoose has always had that extra touch of magic. The Irish and the swathe of green has never quite matched this, but as noted in Chapter 2, provided the very first Boeing 747 'jumbo jet' to land in Wales on 3 March 1978. And the travelling Welsh supporters flying to Dublin will probably never match the early March 1968 airlift to and from the Irish capital. The logs at the airport show that there were 150 extra flights bringing supporters back home from Dublin, many of these Cambrian aircraft – the huge Welsh support came to nought though, Ireland beating Wales 9–6. Certainly the 2011 airlift for the Wales *v.* Ireland international on 12 March was one of the least busy for many decades, with just Aer Arann ATRs and a CityJet BAe146 carrying the supporters, doubtless a result of the impact of the Irish banking/economic woes from earlier in the year.

With club rugby competitions also growing in stature, it is not just internationals that attracted extra charter traffic at Rhoose. In May 2002 the Heineken Cup Final was staged at the Millennium Stadium, Leicester and Munster the finalists. A huge number of Munster supporters travelled from Ireland, some in an assorted fleet of Boeing 747-200s, SE-RBH of Transjet, TF-ADF and 'TE of Air Atlanta and one from European Airways, plus several Aer Lingus Airbus A330s. On the weekend of 20 and 21 May 2011, the airport was again 'humming', this time for the double club rugby finals in Cardiff, Harlequins *v.* Stade Francais for the Amlin Cup on the Friday and Northampton Saints *v.* Leinster for the Heineken Cup on the Saturday – an Aigle Azur Airbus

A319 and CityJet RJ85 flew Stade supporters in on the Friday and then on Saturday morning a variety of chartered airliners, including Amsterdam Airlines A320s, OLT Fokker 100 and Neos Air Boeing 737 with Leinster fans. Again a variety of BizJets provided considerable supporting action.

Amidst the arrivals and departures of rugby fans, the teams and players must not be forgotten, particularly the Welsh players who formed the nucleus of the victorious 1971 British Lions tour team to New Zealand and Australia, managed by Welshman John Dawes. Summoned to meet Prime Minister Sir Edward Heath, iconic players such as Gareth Edwards, Barry John, John Bevan, Mervyn Davies and Derek Quinnell, were flown to London aboard Cambrian Airways Viscount G-ALWF, after much jollity and camera posing on the old main apron at Rhoose. Neither have some of the Welsh team been afraid to embrace their fans when travelling to and from Rhoose. Neil Jenkins is remembered at the airport as a particularly generous player for signatures in children's autograph books and for photographs, notably when the Welsh team returned victorious from Paris on 18 March 2001 following an exciting 43–35 victory over France during which Neil had scored four conversions, two penalties, two drop goals and a try, thus becoming the first international player to break the 1,000 international points barrier. Gareth Edwards returned to Rhoose in an official capacity on 26 November 1998 when he formally opened the revamped and rebranded bar in the terminal, the Scrum-Half.

With the excitement of the rugby airlifts the other national game, football, must not be forgotten. Whether it is Cardiff City FC flying to a fixture in the north of England, East Anglia or even Europe (often in a DHC-8 chartered from Air Southwest, also used in March 2011 to fly the Welsh rugby team to Paris), the period 2001–07, when FA Cup finals were played at the Millennium Stadium because Wembley Stadium was being rebuilt, or when the Wales national side went abroad, Rhoose Airport has been the stepping-off or arrival point for many soccer teams and supporters. In February 1972 Norwich City supporters chartered a trio of Air Anglia DC-3s, G-AGJV, 'MPZ and 'NTD, to fly to Rhoose to support their team. Another memorable event was in September 1987 when Wales were playing Denmark in a qualifier match for the Euro 1988 tournament. Denmark were still living their glory days from a superb run in the 1986 World Cup and their visit to Ninian Park helped them on their way to qualification for the following year's competition. At Rhoose the main days of activity were 8 and 10 September, before and after the match – amongst the airlift aircraft were Sterling Airways with their Boeing 727-2J4 OY-SBE and several shiny new SE210 Caravelle 10B's including OY-STI, whilst Maersk Air flew a Boeing 737-300, Star Air with one of their Fokker F27s and LOT with an Ilyushin Il-18. Many other football charters have occurred, probably the most unusual being the Air Moldova Tupolev Tu-134 ER-65707, which arrived direct from Chisinau, the Moldovan capital, on the morning of 4 September 1995. There was just the team, a few officials and supporters on board, part of the small Moldovan contingent on the terraces at the Arms Park on 6 September for the European cup qualifier which Wales won 1–0. Match over, team showered and changed, a bus to the airport and the Tu-134 was on its way home from Rhoose at 2320hrs. For the 2001 FA Cup final at the Millennium Stadium, Liverpool *v.* Arsenal, the Merseyside team flew to Rhoose, including amongst their number one of the top scoring and most popular footballers of the era, Michael Owen. The fact that he scored his side's two goals in a 2–1 victory just added to the excitement, and many supporters and airport staff took the opportunity to applaud the team members as they returned to Rhoose on 13 May for the short flight home.

A sporting event of a much different kind took place in the grounds of Cardiff Castle on 5 August 1970 and involved a week-long melee of aviation activity at Rhoose with supporters and teams. This was the BBC's hugely popular *It's An International Knock Out*. The aircraft involved were Dutch and French and included a Convair 340 belonging to Dutch charter airline Martinair; unlike the turboprop-powered Convair's of Nor-Fly detailed in Chapter 6, these had their original reciprocating engines, which once they had fired up shrouded the whole apron in a cloud of exhaust and sounds reminiscent of the Cambrian Dakota era. Kelvin Lumb, a local enthusiast, was there to witness the arrival of the first Convair 340 PH-CGD (s/n 104) on Sunday 2 August and takes up the story:

Euralair Caravelle on 25 March 1972 on the old southern apron. (Geoff Jones)

Corse Air Caravelle F-BVPZ used by French rugby supporters to fly from Paris Orly to Rhoose on 17 February 1984. Corse Air used the CS flight code that had been used by Cambrian, causing a few surprised looks when it first called up on the radio. (Mike Kemp)

A stellar selection of classic airliners during the 1978 French rugby airlift: Aerotour and Minerve Caravelles and two EAS Vanguards. (Geoff Jones)

For the 19 February 1972 soccer match between Norwich City and Cardiff City, the East Anglian supporters chartered a trio of Air Anglia DC-3s, G-AGJV, 'MPZ and 'NTD to fly to Wales. (Kelvin Lumb)

The Gwent Branch of Air Britain enthusiasts were invited air-side in March 1976 to view the French rugby airlift aircraft at close quarters, in this case Air France Boeing 727 F-BOJD. (Geoff Jones)

The Martinair Convair arrived with passengers/supporters and after they had left for Cardiff the hosties from the flight were wandering around in the terminal building looking for something to do. I got chatting and offered to drive them to Cardiff for a tour of the city, which to my great shock they accepted. They really enjoyed the quick visit and I returned them in time for their planned return positioning flight to Ostend. A few days later after the 'It's An International Knockout' was over they returned to Rhoose again to ferry their first load of passengers back to Ostend – I happened to be there and was offered a flight to Ostend as there was a free seat. I shot off home to Rhoose village to collect my passport, ringing my mum first to give her time to hunt down the passport and for dad to warm the car engine for a quick return back to the airport. Back at Rhoose Airport I quickly collected a ticket, dashed through customs and on to the Convair which was ready and waiting to go. On arrival at Ostend the passengers were soon off, it was then a quick wander around the tarmac and a kick of the tyres before re-boarding for the positioning flight empty back to Rhoose – only this time I was able to sit in the jump seat in the cockpit. What a flight! On arrival at Rhoose I went through customs only to find that my passport had expired! After a few stern words from the officials about how serious this was and how did I manage to leave the country in the first place, I was back home in Rhoose. What memories of a never to be repeated era!

IT'S A KNOCK OUT 1970 ITINERARY

31 Jul	F-BHMR DC-6, Aeromaritime fm Paris Le Bourget @ 12.09, returning @ 18.08
1 Aug	PH-SAD Fokker F27, NLM fm Amsterdam @ 17.28, returning @ 18.02
2 Aug	F-BGSK DC-6, Aeromaritime fm Paris Le Bourget
	PH-CGD Convair 340, Martinair fm Southend @ 17.00, returning to Ostend @ 17.58
	PH-MAN Douglas DC-9, Martinair fm Amsterdam @ 23.18, returning @ 00.15
5 Aug	PH-MAL Convair 580, Martinair fm Amsterdam @ 18.11, to Dublin @ 18.48
6 Aug	PH-SAD Fokker F27, NLM from and to Amsterdam
	PH-CGD Convair 340, Martinair did three rotations to and from Amsterdam/Ostend
	PH-DNW Douglas DC-9, KLM from Amsterdam @ 16.37, returned to Milan @ 18.00

Awash with visiting aircraft, the old runway 12/22 was utilised for parking the tens of visiting aircraft for the Rugby World Cup Final in Cardiff on 6 November 1999 (Malcolm Bradbury)

This large Airbus A300 B2, F-BUAE, flown by the French domestic airline Air Inter, arrived with supporters for the March 1988 French rugby airlift. (Geoff Jones)

French rugby team and officials arrive at Rhoose from Paris Orly on 15 March 1996 aboard chartered AOM French Airlines Douglas DC-10-30 F-BTDE. (Cardiff Airport)

The Rugby Union World Cup hosted by the WRU in Cardiff in October and November 1999 was another major event to entice large numbers of visiting aircraft to Rhoose. The final on 8 November between France and Australia attracted one of the largest influxes of visiting aircraft. Unfortunately the final did not live up to the excitement of the semi-finals, Australia beating France 35–12.

One of the most recent and significant sporting airlifts seen at Rhoose was between 27 September and 3 October 2010 for the biennial Ryder Cup golf tournament which was held at the Celtic Manor Resort near Newport. The US team, including Tiger Woods, arrived at Rhoose direct from Atlanta, Georgia, on Monday 27 September aboard a chartered British Airways Boeing 777-236ER, G-VIIC, which was followed later in the day by the Sun Country Airlines (a US schedule and charter airline based at Minneapolis–St Paul in Minnesota) Boeing 737-8Q8W N809SY. There followed a large influx of BizJets, plus a few helicopters, many of the BizJets routing in direct from US points of departure – but the anticipated long line-up on the disused runway 12/22 did not materialise, many of the aircraft dropping off then leaving.

The first display – of sorts – at Rhoose was in 1960 as part of the events associated with the London to Cardiff Air Race and Welsh Air Rally that year. As well as the race to Rhoose and several races starting and finishing at Rhoose (see Chapter 10), the RAF's Black Arrows formation aerobatic team performed. They were founded in 1955, and at Rhoose a group of seven Hawker Hunters performed, from 111 Squadron's base at RAF Wattisham in Suffolk.

Welsh British Lions players at Rhoose in 1971 after the successful Lions tour to New Zealand who flew from Rhoose to London to meet the Prime Minister aboard Cambrian's Viscount G-ALWF. Those pictured include John Dawes, Gareth Edwards and Derek Quinnell. (Austin J. Brown)

Opposite from top

An Aer Lingus B737-400 EI-CDH arrives on stand in February 1994 to airlift Welsh rugby supporters to Dublin. (Mike Kemp)

Lockheed L1011 Tristar G-BBAI and two others of the type during the airlift of Welsh rugby supporters to Dublin on 29 February 1996. (Malcolm Bradbury)

The Heineken Cup Final in Cardiff on 24 May 2002 between Munster and Leicester saw a huge influx of Munster supporters flying to Rhoose, some in Transjet Boeing 747 SE-RBH. (Malcolm Bradbury)

When the Wales *v.* Denmark soccer international was played at Ninian Park in September 1987 Danish supporters used a varied fleet of chartered aircraft, including this Sterling Boeing 727 OY-SBE. (Kelvin Lumb)

Martinair from Holland were chartered to fly It's an International Knock Out teams to Rhoose in August 1970 in the Convair CV-340 PH-CGD. (Kelvin Lumb)

1960's London–Cardiff Air Race event featured an air display at Rhoose – the Black Arrows Hawker Hunter display team performed. (Via N. Williams)

1 A fine study of Cambrian's Pionair G-ALXL on the apron at Rhoose on 4 August 1962. (Mike Hooks)

2 One of the first CP Air DC-8 flights from Rhoose to Toronto on 1 July 1977. (Malcolm Bradbury)

3 Viscount G-ALWF parked on the play-pen to the west of the old control tower. (Austin Brown)

4 March 1979 and British Airways BAC1-11 Super One Eleven (Srs. 510ED) G-AVMK departs Rhoose to re-enter service based at Birmingham. (Geoff Jones)

5 In May 1990 this Boeing 747-212B N726PA *Clipper Cathay* of Pan Am diverted in, unable to land at London Heathrow. (Mike Kemp)

Opposite from top

6 The end of the Viscount era at Rhoose; five examples lined up and awaiting disposal in May 1980. (Geoff Jones)

7 In August 1979, Aer Turas Canadair CL-44J EI-BGO, c/n 09, ex-TF-LLH, was chartered to move a consignment of car components – access to its cargo deck is by the characteristic-swing opening tail. (Kelvin Lumb)

8 Airport Director Eddie Maloney greets Pope John Paul II on his visit to Wales on 28 May 1982. (Eddie Maloney Collection)

9 Nelson Mandela arrives in June 1998 greeted by Peter Hain MP and county officials, en route to Cardiff. (Cardiff Airport)

10 Aer Lingus was the launch customer for the Fokker F.27 Friendship – first of the fleet EI-AKA St Fintan was delivered on 19 November 1958, replacing DC-3s on the airline's services to Rhoose, pictured here in 1962. (Mike Hooks)

11 Five former BA B747-200s stored at Rhoose prior to their disposal. (Malcolm Bradbury)

12 Bringing Danish supporters to Cardiff for the September 1987 Wales *v*. Denmark football international, Sterling Caravelle 10B OY-STI is seen just crossing the boundary fence on finals for runway 30. (Kelvin Lumb)

13 16 August 1992 at about 09.00 and Rhoose is humming – a Manx Jetstream 31 G-WENT is at the hold ready to depart to Dublin; Britannia 767-204 G-BRIG positioning in from Luton ready for an Orlando flight; Columbus 737-33A CS-TKD and Inter European 737-3Y0 G-BGNL loading prior to both departing to Faro and Balkan Holidays Tu-154B ready to push back, its destination Varna. (Malcolm Bradbury)

14 European's three BAC1-11s and the airline's smartly dressed flight attendants used Rhoose as a base for airline publicity photos in October 1994. (Cardiff Airport)

15 Thomsonfly and its predecessor airlines have been one of the longest continually operating airlines at Rhoose – this Boeing 737-800 G-FDZF is rotating off runway 30 in 2010. (Geoff Jones)

16 The arrival in the UK direct from Seattle of British Airways' first Boeing 777-336ER (G-STBA) on 10 July 2010 for pre-service entry fitting out at BAMC. (Richard Baker)

17 One of many visits by the RAF's Red Arrows, on the evening of 30 May 1997 when they were flying Hawks and are about to run and break before landing. (Malcolm Bradbury)

18 Airtours leased this Air New Zealand Boeing 747-200 ZK-NZZ in 1998, seen here lifting off from runway 30 at the start of its nine-hour flight to Orlando. (Geoff Jones)

19 In May 1998 Emperor Akihito and Empress Michiko of Japan start their state visit to Wales at Rhoose Airport, flying in on Queens Flight BAe146 ZE701. (Cardiff Airport)

Left 20 Neil Jenkins poses with young fans outside the arrivals hall at Rhoose after the Welsh rugby team return from their 43 35 victory over France in Paris in March 2001. (Malcolm Bradbury)

Below 21 BH Air–Balkan Holidays Airbus A320 LZ-BHD. The airline took over from other Bulgarian operators that had flown charters from Rhoose for many years. (Geoff Jones)

22 The airline bmibaby operated scheduled low-fare flights between October 2002 and October 2011, using its fleet of Boeing 737-300s. (Geoff Jones)

23 British Regional Embraer EMB-145 (G-EMBA) with 'Dove' tail colours on the main apron at Rhoose in 2002. (Geoff Jones)

24 Robin HR.200 and Piper PA-28R on the light aircraft apron at Rhoose in 2005. (Geoff Jones)

25 Controversy regarding the surface of Bristol's runway during resurfacing led to a mass diversion of easyJet A319s on 6 January 2007. (Malcolm Bradbury)

26 Diminutive Piper L-4H Cub (G-AJAD) departs runway 30 in September 2007, with a German DHC-8 (Cirrus Airlines) and RAF jets beyond, illustrating the diverse range of craft handled. (Geoff Jones)

27 Derby Airways Canadair C-4 Argonaut G-ALHS waits at the hold for runway 31 on 4 August 1962. (Mike Hooks)

28 Canadian charter airline Zoom operated from Rhoose to Toronto for two seasons. *City of Ottawa* C-GZUM is shown in September 2007 before the airline's failure in 2008. (Geoff Jones)

29 flybe DHC-8 Series 400 'Dash 8' taxies to stand in 2009 – flybe have a growing presence at Rhoose, claiming to be Europe's 'Number One Regional Airline'. (Geoff Jones)

30 On the steps of their chartered British Airways Boeing 777, the US team arrive at Rhoose from Atlanta, Georgia in September 2010 for the Ryder Cup golf tournament held at the Celtic Manor Resort, Newport. The glare of the Welsh sun is obviously too much for several team members including Tiger Woods! (European Tour)

31 Europe Airpost B737-300 F-GZTA rotates from runway 30 returning to Paris Orly during the March 2010 French rugby airlift. (Geoff Jones)

32 The Aer Lingus colours returned to Rhoose in 2010 when Aer Arann struck a franchise deal and started operating as Aer Lingus Regional. ATR-72 EI-REO is seen here departing runway 30 for the return flight to Dublin. (Geoff Jones)

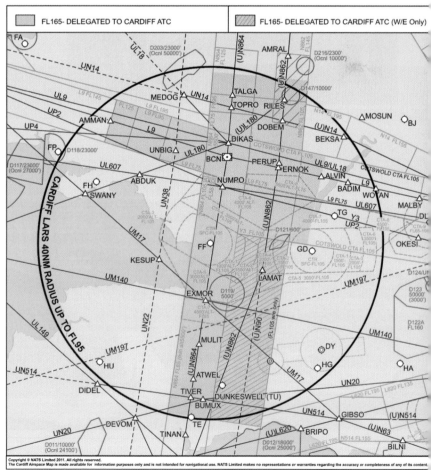

33 Airspace delegated to Cardiff in 2011. (NATS via Malcolm Bradbury)

British- and French-registered airliners give a cosmopolitan mix to March 1980's French rugby airlift, including an EAS Vickers Vanguard. (Geoff Jones)

They still hold the record for the most aircraft flown in close aerobatic formation – twenty-two aircraft – but were disbanded in 1961. Also at this event were four Hunting Jet Provosts from the RAF's Central Flying School at Little Rissington, Gloucestershire, and an Olympia glider demonstration.

Eddie Maloney, the airport director between 1968 and 1983 (see Chapter 9), assisted by the then chairman of the airport board Bob Read and clerk to the board Peter Davey, was responsible for organising three open days with air displays at Rhoose in 1976, 1977 and 1979, always a tricky feat at an operational civil airport which had to continue to operate its scheduled services. The South Wales public flooded to the airport in their thousands, the first event in 1976 attracting an estimated 70,000 people to see a visit from a Dan-Air DH Comet IV, the RAF's Red Arrows performance and much more. In those days 'The Reds' were flying Folland Gnat jets from their base at RAF Kemble in Gloucestershire. From their formation in 1965 through to 1979, Folland Gnats were the team's equipment until the first Hawks arrived for the 1980 season. The Rhoose open day was repeated for the twenty-fifth anniversary of the opening of the airport for commercial services on 8 May 1977, with Fleet Air Arm Firefly (WB271) and the Hurricane and Spitfire (PZ865 and P7350 respectively) and Dan-Air Comet IV G-AROV thrilling the crowds – surprise arrivals from Lelystad in Holland were five Martinair Flying Club Fuji FA-200s. On Sunday 6 May 1979, for the third time, aircraft ancient and modern, including the RAF's Battle of Britain Memorial Flight (Lancaster, Spitfire and Hurricane), aerobatic displays by Richard Goode in his Stampe biplane (G-OODE), Pitts Special aerobatics (G-BBOH) and a Dragon Rapide (G-AIDL) were some of the attractions. Whilst all this was going on Britannia Airways got a Boeing 737-200 away and Dan-Air their Viscount G-BCZR.

The Red Arrows have visited Rhoose on several occasions since, one such occasion on 15 May 1999 in connection with a publicity exercise by Saab who were promoting one of their new Saab Concept cars at the time. Celebrities have also appeared at the airport, television weather presenter Siân Lloyd being one in 2002, when promoting ski holidays for the following winter with the airport's sales and marketing director Caroline Godfrey (see Chapter 6). School children have always been welcome to the airport and in March 1999 one group arrived as part of charity Action Research, complete with Paddington Bear and his battered suitcase. More recently the sight of the airport's firemen, stripped to the waist and pecs proud, sent some pulses racing as air traffic controller and keen photographer Malcolm Bradbury photographed them in 2006 and 2009 for a charity calendar on behalf of Ty Hafan Children's Hospice.

In May 1969 the *Daily Mail* Transatlantic Air Race involved Rhoose, celebrating the fiftieth anniversary of Alcock and Brown's epic 1919 first transatlantic non-stop crossing from Newfoundland to Clifden in Galway, Ireland. With the objective to get from the top of the Empire State Building in New York to the top of the Post Office Tower in London, the fastest time of just over four hours was recorded by an RAF Phantom jet. In a different class, one of the aircraft participating was an ex-Irish Air Corps Spitfire Mk IX Trainer G-AVAV, from Strathallan, which made an unscheduled visit to the club apron on 7 May 1969, flown by an Elstree-based chief flying instructor John Schooling. Another event at Rhoose on 22 May 1993 was POLAIR 93, the Police National Air Rally which attracted an assortment of thirteen different light aircraft, presumably flown by off-duty police officers. Most recently was the Jodel Fly-In on 11 June 2011 to celebrate the life of Geoff Claxton (see Chapter 10).

In October 1994, marginally 'a display', was the arrival at Rhoose from Filton of a trio of BAC1-11s of EAL in their striking new red and white livery. Newly branded European Air Charter, part of European Aviation Ltd, were Bournemouth-based and specialised in air charter and operated schedules for a short while for Air Bristol, their large fleet of ex-British Airways BAC1-11s and flight attendants in striking red and white colours. After the photo shoot for publicity purposes on the apron at Rhoose, the three BAC1-11s, G-AVMH, 'K and 'N, took off for a rendezvous over the Bristol Channel with the Jet Ranger helicopter G-BFJW for an air-to-air photo shoot.

The end of another era at Rhoose occurred on 29 June 2008 when the last commercial passenger carrying Douglas DC-3/Dakota flight operated from the airport. Due to the changing

Left Weathergirl Siân Lloyd, assisted by Cardiff Airport's Sales and Marketing Director Caroline Godfrey, help to promote Skiers World holidays that were to be available from the airport in winter 2002/3. (Cardiff Airport)

Below Line-up for the third air display organised by Eddie Maloney in May 1979. (Peter R. March)

Above The airport Fire and Rescue Service pose with make-up artists Karen Brown and Sara Kyte (from H'art and Soul Beauty Salon) in September 2008 for the 2009 Fireman's Calendar sold in aid of Ty Hafan Children's Hospice. It was the second time this calendar had been produced, with the first released in 2006 – another is planned for 2012. (Malcolm Bradbury)

Right Probably the last commercial Douglas DC-3 operation at Rhoose on 29 June 2008, when Air Atlantique did several enthusiast flights from the airport using G-AMPY, marked as RAF KK116. (Geoff Jones)

CAA regulations, Coventry-based Air Atlantique with their small fleet of airworthy DC-3s that they used for passenger pleasure flights around the UK would have had to be extensively modified to comply with these new regulations. They decided this would be uneconomic so the summer 2008 season was organised with enthusiast flights from many UK commercial airports including Rhoose. Their DC-3 G-AMPY (a former Starways aircraft), painted in RAF colours as KK116, flew hundreds of enthusiasts on nostalgia flights that weekend, the characteristic drone of its Pratt & Whitney radial engines, so familiar in the Cambrian era, reverberating again over the green acres of Porthkerry Park, the Knap and the viaduct, as Air Atlantique celebrated with this 'queen of the skies'. They also flew their DH.104 Dove (G-DHDV/VP981) to Rhoose that day as a crew ferry for the Dak.

8

RUNWAY EXTENSIONS AND INFRASTRUCTURE

The first runway extension at Rhoose was a south-western lengthening of runway 04/22 from the original wartime length of 3,700ft to 4,534ft during the tenure of the RAF's 7AGS around 1943–44. Runway 22 (now disused and used for aircraft parking during large events) was the runway of choice before the 1970 extension of 13/31, provided the wind was from the south-west or west. Even with 4,534ft of runway, some of the heavily laden Derby Airways Canadair Argonauts and Euravia Constellations, which were an early 1960s highlight flying charter passengers from Rhoose to Mediterranean resorts, would trundle off the end of runway 22, almost aircraft carrier-like, clawing their way into the skies (see Chapter 6). In the early days of commercial operations the facilities were rudimentary – no VOR (VHF omni-directional range) or more sophisticated equipment, just a SBA (Standard Beam Approach) and basic search radar in bad weather. Listening to the Rhoose tower radio frequency on a VHF receiver (Gaüer or Shorrocks were the only options for enthusiasts then) you could hear the controller talking to the pilots: 'your range is 5 miles, you should be at an altitude of 2,000ft, you are slightly right of the centre line.' This went on until the 'decision height' was reached and hopefully the pilot had established visual contact with the runway and its runway lead-in lights (see below).

The next most noticeable improvement was the erection in early 1954 of the T2 hangar that became Cambrian Airways' maintenance facility and refurbishment of the small main apron and southern taxiway – later in the 1950s the main aircraft parking apron was extended south-westwards forming a relatively large and uninterrupted strip from Glamorgan Flying Club's building through to the hangar. The new terminal building was also built around this time, embracing some of the former wartime buildings as its core, but with a smart new frontage and paved walkways with some pergola-style coverings. The former Nashcrete buildings were an asset and utilised in a variety of ways as Cambrian's cargo shed, crew rooms, offices and canteens. The watchtower, located to the north of the old main apron, was refurbished around 1961, with a larger and more user friendly VCR (visual control unit) atop it. The next big capital investment in 1962–63 was the 'play-pen', a large overflow aircraft parking area to the west of the control tower and adjoining the taxiway that led from the main apron to the threshold of runway 12. This was used for the growing number of corporate aircraft that were visiting Rhoose, and also as an overflow for larger commercial aircraft, including Cambrian. This is still in existence, used for resident light aircraft parking. The visiting public – and Rhoose was a popular destination for day-trippers – could also get up close and personal with the aircraft from behind the chest high wooden fence that separated land-side from air-side. An ice cream or cool drink sat on the metal stacker chairs dotted around the public enclosure and watching the aircraft come and go was a

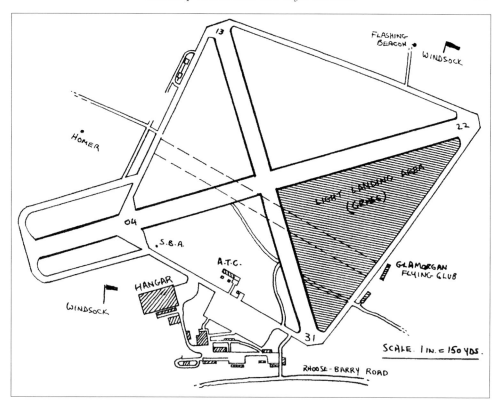

Sketch of the airport prepared in 1958 for the PFA rally at Rhoose. (Geoff Jones Collection)

The airport terminal area, looking north-eastwards, just prior to the arrival of Cambrian Air Services in April 1954. (Via N. Williams)

Crowds of spectators visited Rhoose to look at the aircraft in the 1960s; here an Aer Lingus Viscount is the centre of attention. (Cardiff Airport)

Opposite from top

View south from the control tower around 1962. Cambrian's maintenance hangar can be seen on the right, with the terminal building on the left, behind the left-hand of the two Cambrian Dakotas. The stack of Rhoose cement works can also be seen. (Gary Hilliard)

Airport Commandant 1954–69, Mickey Ogden (right) with Sir James Lyons (centre), Lord Mayor of Cardiff and airport manager for two decades from the mid-1950s, on a visit to Filton to see work on the BAC Concorde. (Michael Ogden)

Councillors and officers of the airport and owners Glamorgan CC in 1965 in front of the main terminal building. Second from the right is Airport Commandant Mr C.V. Ogden; behind and to his right is the tall figure of future airport director Eddie Maloney. In the back row to the far left is Llew John, a senior engineer employed by Glamorgan CC. (Cardiff Airport)

popular pastime in the pre-security ridden era of the 1950s and 1960s at Rhoose. Pleasure flights at the adjacent Glamorgan Flying Club in anything from a Tiger Moth or Auster to the more modern Cessna 172 and Piper Tripacer were another attraction.

Between 1954 and 1969 Mickey Ogden was airport commandant, and on 15 August 1962 he discussed with the airport committee a draft agreement with the Air Ministry to operate the airport for seven years from 1 April 1965, during which time the council could not employ any contractor for capital works without the consent of the ministry. The ministry were also to provide air traffic control, etc., whilst the council were to maintain the runway 'visual equipment'. Llewellyn Heycock was the first chairman of this committee with Thomas Evans (Pontardawe) as vice-chair – Percy Smith (Llantwit Major) chaired some of the meetings. It was estimated that the airport's assets totalled £75,000 and that should the authority close the airport, the ministry had the right to claim these assets. It was at the committee meeting on 18 February 1963 that the development possibility of either extending the runway or building a new 7,000ft 'east–west runway' was first aired, and also surprisingly that jets would be excluded. In October 1964 Wing Commander C.V. 'Mickey' Ogden was offered the job of airport director with a Mr Jimmy Lyons – later Sir James Lyons, who also became Lord Mayor of Cardiff – as manager. Wing Commander Ogden retired in 1969.

The next big event at Rhoose was in 1965 when Glamorgan County Council took over control of the airport from the Ministry of Aviation in a ceremony attended by Rt Hon. Roy Jenkins

Part of the new radar unit is craned in to position in April 1969, prior to the opening of the new control tower the following year. (Cardiff Airport)

The first jet airliner lands at Rhoose on 9 March 1970, an Aer Lingus Boeing 737. (Cardiff Airport)

County Alderman George Adams and representatives of main contractor Tarmac Construction lay the foundation stone for the new terminal building on 31 March 1971. (Cardiff Airport)

The official opening of the new terminal by HRH Duke of Edinburgh on 11 December 1972. (Eddie Maloney Collection)

On St David's Day 1986, the French are in town – seen in this aerial view looking west over the airport towards Aberthaw. (Cardiff Airport)

MP, then Minister of Aviation, together with senior representatives of Glamorgan County Council. An over £5 million investment in the airport was announced soon after for airport upgrades that would transform Rhoose into a major international airport capable of handling modern jet airliners. By July 1965 preliminary steps had been taken to extend runway 13/31, plus construction of a new terminal had begun. Nevertheless, in January 1966 it was agreed to build a covered way from the departure gates to the edge of the apron and in September refurbishment of the restaurant in the terminal commenced at a cost of £10,000. An unsuccessful bid was made by NCP to take over control of car parking at the airport and Cambrian Airways' attempt to create their own departure lounge and baggage-handling area was also rejected. A small new hangar to the south-west of Cambrian's, for light aircraft use, was built at a cost of £4,106, with the council carrying out the basic work. By April 1968 a new airport director was to be appointed; there were eighty-nine applicants, thirty-seven of whom had some experience of airport management and of the others one was an Olympic Airways pilot – this was when Eddie Maloney took up his tenure as director, arriving after a stint at Bristol Airport, through Rhoose's most dynamic metamorphism, until his retirement in 1983 (see Chapter 9).

The construction of the new control tower on the eastern perimeter of the airport was part of a bold move that would eventually see the whole focus of the airport shift from the small, somewhat parochial facilities on the south side and adjacent to the Barry–Rhoose road, to the huge new complex that characterises the airport today. The start of developments of the runway and new tower/terminal building spelt the end of the infrequently used grass runway (aligned 09/27), whose threshold was close to the old fire station and approximately in the position of the current control tower. It had been used occasionally by commercial aircraft – mainly Dakotas and Pionairs – when there was a strong westerly wind, and the tail-wheel Dakotas could be landed more safely directly into wind. A major part of this significant capital investment was the lengthening of the 13/31 runway to the south-east towards Porthkerry and the need to divert the main B4265 road in a large loop, south-east around the runway's threshold, to enter Rhoose village near to the old pump. The new 7,000ft runway opened for business early in 1970, followed soon after by the new VCR. Landing a Boeing 737 on this new runway cost £41 12s in landing fees, a BAC1-11 £35 4s, and a Viscount £24 in 1971, and in August both Dan-Air and Court Line were actively seeking landing-fee reductions. An application to construct a petrol filling station on land in front of the new terminal building was made but rejected, and sadly none of the high-street banks was prepared to open a branch in the new terminal.

The next part of the strategic plan was the construction of the new terminal building, the foundation stone for which was laid on 31 March 1971 by County Alderman George Adams, helped by other managers and dignitaries, plus representatives from the main contractor, Tarmac. Just over a year later, on 11 December 1972, the huge and ultra-modern facility, combined with a vast new aircraft-parking apron, was officially opened by HRH Prince Philip, the Duke of Edinburgh – Eddie Maloney described the duke as 'very knowledgeable but testy'. The duke arrived at noon and officially opened the airport, during which the Bishop of Llandaff dedicated the airport, followed by a luncheon in a specially erected marquee. At 1410hrs the duke set off on a tour of inspection of the new facilities, and at 1500hrs, with the ceremonies over, he departed in an Andover of the Queen's Flight. The airport was still only handling fewer than 200,000 passengers per annum during the first few years after the new terminal's opening, but the facilities were in place, including new freight sheds, a new fire station and fuel farm. The old terminal on the south side became an enclave for club and private flying, the former Cambrian hangar still in use for BAS aircraft maintenance.

Air Traffic Control

Throughout Rhoose's civilian history Air Traffic Control (ATC) service has been provide by a government body with the current ATC provider being the part-privatised company NATS. Malcolm Bradbury, a controller here between 1990 and 2008, and still working for NATS, guides us through the history of this most important facility, which not only embraces the airport itself but air space surrounding and above the airport. Rhoose is always referred to as 'Cardiff' by ATC, but to maintain consistency with the rest of the book I continue to use 'Rhoose'.

Visual approach slope indicator lights were installed at the runway touch-down points in 1963 and became operational on 11 November. In 1965 controlled airspace (non-rule 21) was first established in the vicinity of the airport, and linked the airport with the airway Amber 25 at Brecon to the north, Bristol to the east and then the latter with airway Green One at Chepstow – this airspace was known as the Bristol Channel Control Area. This was short-lived and disestablished in the early 1980s, replaced by a Special Rules Zone which encompassed the airport with its own Special Rules Area protecting the runway 30 approach, the prevailing landing direction – the reciprocal runway 12 was not afforded similar airspace. The Special Rules Airspace was reclassified as Class 'D' airspace, which, following several incidents coupled with an increase in traffic, now embraced the runway 12 approach also.

In 1998 the ATC unit was delegated by the London Air Traffic Control Centre at West Drayton to provide a wider ATC coverage up to FL115 (11,500ft) between TALGA and EXMOR and AMMAN and ALVIN (see Fig. 33 in plate section). This task was extended vertically in July 2003 to FL165 and southwards to a position overhead Exeter Airport. The ATC unit at Rhoose also provides an approach-radar service to MOD St Athan, 4 miles to the west of the airport. This allows semi-autonomous operations with a Local Flying Zone established around

The sad sight of the old control tower being demolished in 1970 after the new one, visible in the distance, was commissioned. (Kelvin Lumb)

Malcolm Bradbury at work in front of one of the radar screens used to help control aircraft using the airport or transiting its airspace. (Malcolm Bradbury)

Cambrian Dakota G-AMSX in front of the rudimentary watch-tower at Rhoose in the 1950s. (Garry Hilliard)

Controllers in the VCR (visual control room) in August 1997: Keith Menkin (ATC General Manager), Albert Harrison (Airport Director) and a visitor. (Cardiff Airport)

Aerial view of the airport terminal and aprons at the time of the Wales *v.* Denmark football international in September 1987. (Cardiff Airport)

St Athan enabling aircraft to arrive and depart St Athan VFR (Visual Flight Rules) by entering and exiting the Control Zone via the Visual Reference Point (VRP) at Nash Point and without having to obtain clearance from Rhoose ATC during the hours of watch of St Athan ATC.

On 31 August 2008 a major change took place in the controlled airspace structure in the vicinity of Rhoose and Bristol airports when an airspace change proposal, submitted jointly by the two airports and approved by the Civil Aviation Authority (CAA) following an extensive consultation process, was introduced. Need for this was driven by the necessity for a joint approach to airspace utilisation in the vicinity of both airports due to increasing numbers of public transport movements generated by low-fare airline Go (taken over by easyJet in August 2002) at Bristol and, to a lesser extent, following bmibaby's establishment at Rhoose in 2003. An enhanced safety environment resulted, and Standard Instrument Departures (SIDs) and Standard Instrument Arrival Routes (STARS) for both airports were introduced.

To operate these varying and evolving air traffic services, the Rhoose-based controllers have used increasingly sophisticated equipment, but home for these have been two control towers topped off with their characteristic glasshouse-style VCR, the old, converted watchtower on the airport's south side, demolished in 1970, and the new and current tower part of the terminal complex. This current tower also houses the airport's administration offices.

The main approach aid to the airport was the Standard Beam Approach (SBA). This was an approach developed during the Second World War and an early forerunner of the ILS (Instrument Landing System). HOMER, a direction-finding aid, was also utilised and a Non-Directional Beacon (NDB). Standard Beam Approach was replaced with a Decca 424 3cm Search Radar and HOMER by Automatic Direction Finding (ADF) equipment as funds were made available in the run up to the 1958 Empire Games in Cardiff. The Decca 424 radar enabled controllers to 'talk an aircraft down' to within half a mile from the runway and to provide a limited surveillance service.

In 1965 a Plessey AR1 10cm surveillance radar was installed at the airport which enabled a radar service to be provided to a range of 40 mile radius from the airport. In 1973 an ILS was installed for use by aircraft landing on runway 31 (as it was then), the Decca 424 radar continuing in use for aircraft arriving on runway 13, which did not have an ILS. However, with the introduction of an ILS on runway 12 in November 1985, the Decca 424 radar was withdrawn from service. The AR1 radar was replaced in 1983 by a Marconi/Cossor system which enabled secondary surveillance system radar data to be fed into the unit from the NATS radar site at Clee Hill in Shropshire. The year 1991 saw a further upgrade with a Marconi Messenger

SSR system being installed along with a replacement Marconi S511 Primary Radar Aerial positioned 'back-to-back' atop the control tower building. This was the first time that Rhoose had been equipped with an airport-based SSR. The Clee Hill radar is still being utilised to supplement the airport's radar when the latter is on maintenance. The airport's radar was further updated in 2010 with a Thales 2000 Primary Surveillance Radar and a Thales RSM970S Mode 'S' Secondary Surveillance Radar. The aerials for this equipment are stack mounted and occupy a new site south of runway 12/30. It may all sound complicated, but the new equipment enables Rhoose to boast some of the best and most up to date ATC equipment available, adding to the airport's excellent safety record, plus on-time arrivals and departures for its passengers. The ATC equipment, radar, ILS, NDB, DME, VDF, RT communications equipment, transmissometers, in fact most equipment used by ATC, is looked after by a small group of NATS engineers who work as a team with the ATC staff.

Back in 1974, coincident with local government reorganisation, the airport was taken over by a consortium of West, Mid and South Glamorgan county councils and renamed Cardiff-Wales Airport, and under a government white paper in 1978 Rhoose was designated the official regional airport for the south-west of Britain, although dropped as official policy four years later. In 1977 Gordon Parsons first became involved with the airport, appointed airport accountant by the then airport treasurer, who was also Treasurer of West Glamorgan County Council. Whilst the airport director and his operational/administrative staff were located at Rhoose, other services such as legal, architectural, estates, engineering and finance were provided by the three county councils – financial services were provided by West Glamorgan. Gordon remembers this era:

> At the time the airport was handling 250,000 passengers per annum and was losing £1.5 million per annum, a loss funded by the ratepayers of the three CCs. My task was to establish whether the airport could ever be profitable. Our forecasts indicated that the airport could break even in 1985/86, but the success story was that we *got in to the black*, just, in 1984/85 and continued to make contributions to the coffers of the three CCs thereafter.

Under the Airports Act of 1986 the airport was transformed in to a limited company, with all the shares held by the three county councils. Gordon Parsons did most of the financial groundwork to enable the company to be set up, and was then appointed company secretary and finance director to the airport company.

On 11 December 1986 Pam and Eddy Percy became the half-millionth passengers to use the airport in the year (the first time such a milestone was reached) – the event was celebrated by the couple with Airport Manager Ian Cran, the crew of their Britannia Airways Boeing 737 and a representative from Thomson Holidays. (Cardiff Airport)

Another mix of traffic on 13 January 1992: Manx Jetstream G-BSIX, Piper PA-30 G-ASSR, Britannia B737 G-BJCV and the most unusual Air Gambia Boeing 707 EL-AKC. The 707 was en route from Fuerteventura to Manchester when it diverted in the early hours of 12 January. It departed for Manston, Kent, the next day. (Malcolm Bradbury)

This stylised aircraft tail was erected in 1994 to welcome visitors and passengers to Cardiff-Wales Airport. (Geoff Jones)

1985–86 was a special time because a further runway extension to the north-west (the threshold of runway 12) became necessary so that airliners, including the Boeing 747 'jumbo jet', could depart Rhoose with a full load of fuel and passengers for destinations on the eastern seaboard of the USA – this additional 725ft extension cost £1 million, coinciding with the runway heading being redesignated 12/30 due to the earth's magnetic drift. It was opened in 1986. There followed installation of three new air bridges or jet-ways so that passengers could walk from the terminal and into their aircraft without getting wet or wind-blown. These air bridges were officially opened on 1 February 1989 by Lord Cledwyn Hughes of Penrhos, and the first aircraft to use them was an Inter European Boeing 737 G-BNGL the following day. In the early 1990s a multi-million-pound upgrade to the terminal building, which included a large extension on the south-eastern end, mainly a new arrivals and baggage-reclaim facility, was constructed. With runway 12/30 now in use for the majority of commercial operations, the cross runway 04/22 was little used, mainly by private and club aircraft when wind direction dictated a preference for its use.

Another notable year was 1992 – Rhoose's fiftieth anniversary – followed in 1994 by the landmark of 1 million passengers in a year for the first time. In autumn 1994 a new approach road to the airport terminal was opened. Access via the roundabout close to the aircraft parking apron (and a popular place for aircraft watchers to park their cars despite the yellow lines) was closed to all but those going to and from the freight sheds. At the same time a new 'welcome' sign was erected in the shape of an aircraft tail fin with 'Welcome to Cardiff-Wales Airport: Croeso i Faes Awyr Cymru Caerdydd' on it. This has since been removed with modifications to the airport approach and vehicle setting-down or picking-up arrangements.

The early 1990s was also an important time at Rhoose because British Airways was persuaded, against heavy competition, to build its new maintenance base at the airport (see Chapter 12). Central government was also placing obstacles on the development of Rhoose and other publicly owned airports in the early 1990s, which proved a massive frustration. The government reduced the necessary approvals to borrow money, but it was not that the government funded the works, but nevertheless they gradually withdrew borrowing approvals. So it was no surprise that as a result of local government reorganisation in the mid-1990s, Rhoose Airport was privatised, bought by TBI plc in April 1995. In 2001 Gordon Parsons retired as managing director of the airport.

TBI made significant investments in the airport, simultaneous with a very large increase in passenger numbers (see Appendix 2) and operating profit; in the period 1995 to 2003 passenger numbers increased by over 80 per cent, with scheduled passenger numbers increasing by over 400 per cent – operating profits also increased, by over 150 per cent. By the time of the 2002 sixtieth anniversary of the airport, passenger numbers were up to 1.5 million.

In January 2005 Abertis Infrastructuras SA acquired TBI. Abertis Airports manage British airport operator TBI through a company owned by Abertis (90 pet cent) and Aena Internacional (10 per cent). The network of TBI's eight international airports are London Luton, Cardiff and Belfast International in the UK; Stockholm Skavsta in Sweden; La Paz, Santa Cruz and Cochabamba in Bolivia; and Orlando Sanford in the USA. It also has partial management

Rhoose's roof-top viewing terrace was a huge asset for spectators until the sad impact of heightened security post-9/11 forced its closure. (Malcolm Bradbury)

'Cutter One' Richard Bailey in 2002, the airport groundsman for many years. (Malcolm Bradbury)

Bristow Helicopters Westland Wessex 60 G-ATCA that crashed on the airport on 9 September 1972, fortunately without loss of life or injury to the crew. (John Mead)

contracts from governments and local authorities involving five further airports in the USA, Hartsfield Jackson Atlanta International (the world's busiest airport by passenger numbers), Bob Hope (Burbank, California), Middle Georgia Regional at Macon, Macon Downtown and Raleigh-Durham International. In 2007 Abertis acquired Desarrollo de Concesiones Aeroportuarias (DCA), a holding company with stakes in fifteen airports in Mexico, Jamaica, Chile and Colombia, the twelve airports in Mexico managed by Grupo Aeroportuario del Pacifico (GAP). In Colombia Abertis Airports manages, through operator Codad, the two runways at El Dorado-Bogota Airport and provides a consultancy service at the Castellón-Costa Azahar airport in Spain.

The old Cambrian maintenance hangar finally came to the end of its useful life. In latter days of the 1990s it was used by private aircraft owners for hangarage. It began to deteriorate and, with no money to spend on costly maintenance, it is alleged that one of the aircraft owners spoke to the airport and said that should any of the structure fall on his aircraft he'd hold the airport liable. That was the final straw and in the summer of 2001 the historic but rotting wartime T2 hangar was demolished. The concrete floor was left in situ and provides open-air parking for light aircraft, overlooked by the 'white house' home of Aeros flying school, the flying club bar/restaurant and the Signature FBO offices. Alongside this is what is known as 'the Norman apron', now also parking for visiting GA aircraft being handled by Signature. A few individual lock-up hangars have also appeared around the edges of this apron for some of the lighter GA aircraft that are now based.

Rhoose has had an impeccable safety record for the whole of its civilian career. There have been many 'incidents' but the only fatalities recorded are to the pilots of light aircraft, first in August 1962 (see Chapter 10) and on the evening of 20 August 1997, when Tiger Moth G-AOBJ set off on an air-to-air photography flight with another Tiger Moth (G-ANFI) and well-known local orthopaedic surgeon David Jenkins received fatal injuries in an unfortunate accident. A couple of the incidents at Rhoose included the Bristow helicopters Westland Wessex G-ATCA on 9 September 1972, when it inexplicably burst in to flames and was written off; on 5 October 1993 when Channel Express Herald freighter G-BEYK lost a nose wheel on landing and blocked the runway for three hours; and then on 1 June 2006 when the RAF Dominie jet XS709 inexplicably ran off the runway and on to the grass when landing.

9

CORPORATE CARDIFF

One of the first corporate operations noted at Rhoose was the summertime basing of the Percival Prentice G-AOKH in the late 1950s. This redoubtable ex-military trainer was painted in the colours of Lamtex Luxury Rugs and would spend many hours flying east and west along the coastline of South Wales, particularly the popular beaches of the Knap (then Cold Knap), Whitmore Bay, Barry Island and Porthcawl, trailing its advertising banner behind it. Such is the power of advertising that it left an indelible mark on my memory, and particularly the brand.

Use of aircraft for corporate purposes had not really developed in the 1950s, but there were quite a few examples of Rhoose being used for the upsurge in aerial mapping and survey work over Wales and south-west England. One of these companies was Meridian Air Maps who used Miles Aerovans for their work, one of which, G-AJKP, operated from the airport in the summer of 1957. Other survey companies that visited Rhoose in the late 1950s and early 1960s included Kemps Aerial Surveys, BKS Air Surveys, Fairey Air Surveys and Hunting Surveys, most of whom used ex-military Avro Anson's (Avro Nineteens) and Dragon Rapides. The Ministry of Transport and Civil Aviation was still responsible for Rhoose and their fleet of aircraft included DH Doves and Percival P.50 Princes, used for liaison visits and for calibration of equipment, and approach and runway lighting.

During the 1960s many companies started using Rhoose to regularly fly their executives on board these 'special' aircraft, making visits to factories and offices in South Wales – the list of early to mid-1960s companies and aircraft types below illustrate how important the DH Dove and Heron were in this market, with the first of the US-built Beech, Piper and Cessna twins starting to make inroads to the market. It also provides a snapshot of the diversity of large corporations that were active in South Wales at the time. Some of these were as follows:

Bass Charrington	Piaggio P.166	G-ARUJ
British Oxygen	Beech 65 Queen Air	G-ARII
British Ropes	Beech 55 Baron	G-ASRV
Davy-Ashmore	Beech 65 Queen Air	G-ARFF
Ferranti Ltd	DH.114 Heron	G-ASCX
Forte Group	Beech Queen Air	G-ASKM
Ind Coope Breweries	DH.104 Dove	G-ARDE
McAlpines	Piaggio P.166	G-ASPC
McVities Biscuits	Miles Gemini	G-AKDJ
	Aero Commander 560	G-ASYA

Airport Commandant Mickey Ogden on the left, with HRH Prince Philip and Lord Lieutenant Sir Cennydd Traherne and his wife in June 1958 just before the opening of the Commonwealth Games. (Michael Ogden)

National Coal Board	DH.104 Dove	G-ARUM
Philip Hill, Higginson, Erlangers Ltd	DH.104 Dove	G-ARHX
Pressed Steel Fisher (Prestair)	Dove and Heron	G-AOFI and G-AMTS
Pye Aviation	Cessna 310	G-ASMD
Shell Mex & BP	PA-30 Twin Comanche	G-ASOB
Tube Investments	DH.114 Heron	G-ANPV
United Steel	PA-23 Apache	G-APMY
	Piaggio P.166	G-APXK

On 21 January 1964 the Minnesota Mining and Manufacturing Corp (3Ms), who had established a factory in South Wales, flew their Lockheed Learstar HB-AMM (s/n 2543) to Rhoose, leaving later in the day for London Gatwick – it was back again on 27 January the following year. This conversion of a Second World War USAAF L-18-56 Lodestar patrol aircraft was the aircraft of choice for executive transport – certainly in the USA – in the late 1950s and early 1960s, a precursor to turboprops and executive jets, whose arrivals were major events at Rhoose. As can be seen from the above tabulation, corporations were using basic piston engine aircraft, but things were changing with the advent of the King Air, a turbine-powered development of the Queen Air. The world of business aviation was changing – four-engine Lockheed Jetstars and North American T-39s were being bought by some high-end corporate users. These were derivatives of military aircraft, but one of the first truly purpose-built and iconic executive jets was Bill Lear's Lear Jet 23, which first flew on 7 October 1963 at Wichita, Kansas. The French Dassault Mystère 20 had flown on 4 May 1963. The arrival of the first executive jet at Rhoose was on 27 January 1966, when Air Hanson's Hawker Siddeley HS125 G-ASNU arrived. Later that year arrival of a Norwegian-registered Lear Jet 23 LN-NPE of air taxi/charter company Busy Bee was a memorable event, marshalled to the new concrete ramp (sometimes called the play-pen) to the west of the old control tower. Busy Bee was founded in 1966 by shipping owner Bjorn Braathen at Oslo's Fornebu Airport using a single Piper PA-23 Aztec. Their Lear

G-ARDE corporate DH104 Dove 6 operated by brewing consortium Ind Coupe, visiting on 27 August 1964. (Geoff Jones)

Piaggio P.166B 'Portofino' G-ASPC with its unusual 'pusher' engines on 25 August 1964, operated by McAlpine Aviation. (Geoff Jones)

A Gulfstream 1 N705G owned by IBM visited on 17 August 1966, a pointer to the way that corporate air travel was progressing. (Geoff Jones)

Cosmetics giant Revlon, with a large factory in South Wales, used their BAC1-11 N767RV for visits from the US to Wales, as here on 18 March 1978. (Geoff Jones)

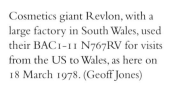

Lord Robens, Chairman of the NCB (National Coal Board), is interviewed by the BBC on 22 October 1966 on his arrival, travelling to visit the site of the Aberfan disaster which had occurred the day before. (Geoff Jones)

Jet 23 was delivered from the US in August 1966 and flew on a charter to Rhoose soon after, on 14 October, stopping for the night and returning to Oslo the next afternoon. If you fly today on Norwegian Air Shuttle, that airline's roots can be traced back directly to Busy Bee. However, statements of 'first' or 'largest' always have to be treated with caution, and it is known that a French-designed and built Morane Saulnier MS.760 Paris jet visited Rhoose some time around 1961–62, and whilst some may argue against the Paris being an 'exec jet', this may have been the first, and also Rhoose's first civil jet arrival. An RAF Vampire T.11 landed on 9 October 1959, probably the 'first' jet arrival.

Several other significant business and corporate aircraft arrivals occurred around this time. What the *Western Mail* described as a 'huge helicopter', a World Wide Helicopters Sikorsky S.58 N871, was based at Rhoose from the 24 to 26 June 1964 whilst lifting a new telecommunications mast in to place at Thornhill near Cardiff. On 4 April 1965 the Ford Motor Company's Grumman G159 Gulfstream 1 (N726G) visited, followed on 17 August 1966 by the visit of another Gulfstream 1 (N705G) belonging to International Business Machines (IBM), a portent of the growing importance of business and corporate aviation at Rhoose. Revlon were another US-based manufacturer to establish a large production facility on one of South Wales' many burgeoning industrial estates, manufacturing cosmetics. This is undoubtedly part of the reason for the visit to Rhoose on 18 March 1978 with their corporate BAC1-11, N767RV – the fact there was a big rugby international in town that day (Wales *v.* France) may also have had something to do with the visit. The BAC1-11 was a familiar aircraft at Rhoose, but not in corporate use, another portent of the development of business aviation with much larger and longer-range aircraft.

One of the saddest times at Rhoose – and the whole of Wales and the UK – was the October 1966 Aberfan disaster. On the morning of Friday 21 October, after a period of very heavy rain, a slag heap on the hillside above the village of Aberfan (4 miles south of Merthyr Tydfil) slid down the hill, engulfing Ynysowen primary school and killing 116 children and twenty-eight adults. World attention focused on this small mining village and every journalist and news organisation needed to be on the spot as quickly as possible to report the story. My memory of this day, then as a Barry Grammar schoolboy, was why could I hear so many aircraft flying over the school to land at Rhoose? At tea time we all found out why, as Rhoose became the focus of a mass influx of air taxis and other aircraft carrying journalists, news teams and help-ers – Doves, Herons, Apaches, Aztecs, Cessna 310/320s, Cessna singles and even a Brantly B2 helicopter were the core of the airlift. By the Saturday afternoon, when it became apparent that the probable cause of the disaster was the instability of a National Coal Board (NCB) slag heap, their president Lord Robens had no alternative but to visit and inspect the scene. He arrived at Rhoose at 1750hrs aboard the NCB Dove G-ARUM, and, whilst transiting through the terminal building, was mobbed by journalists and television crews, all wanting pictures and interviews. Obviously keen to get on his way to Aberfan, and out of the spotlight, Lord Robens granted the BBC a brief interview, which went out live on the six o'clock news from Rhoose Airport, before he was bundled into a car and driven to Aberfan.

Many world-renowned dignitaries, stars and politicians have graced the tarmac at Rhoose over the years. On 6 March 1975 US Secretary of State, Henry Kissinger, who had earned the reputation as a globetrotter, visited in one of the US Presidential Boeing 707s, Air Force One. He was in Wales to visit George Thomas and to then attend a banquet at Cardiff City Hall where James Callaghan, then UK Prime Minister, was given the Freedom of the City. Many other famous names were diligently recorded at Rhoose between September 1968 and

Right A youthful Queen Elizabeth II is greeted by Eddie Maloney in 1969, having arrived in an Andover of the Queen's Flight (XS790). (Eddie Maloney Collection)

Below Henry Kissinger, US Secretary of State, arrives on 6 March 1975 to be greeted by George Thomas (right) and Jim Callaghan before receiving the freedom of the City of Cardiff. (Eddie Maloney Collection)

One of the many College of Air Training (CoAT) Piper PA-23 Apache twins (G-ASDG) that were frequent visitors in the 1960s, undertaking pilot training from their base at Hamble. (Geoff Jones)

September 1983 by airport director Eddie Maloney. Eddie oversaw a capital investment of £5 million, a large amount in the late 1960s. Eddie also kept his hand in at flying, a member of the Glamorgan Flying Club and keen on the Glosair Airtourers they were flying at the time.

Eddie made a point of meeting most of the VIPs that passed through Rhoose and noted meeting the Queen on several occasions, the first being in January 1969 when royalty usually travelled in an Andover of the Queen's Flight. These Andovers were basically Hawker Siddeley HS.748 turboprops. He also met Princess Anne in the autumn of 1969, Princess Margaret and Lord Louis Mountbatten just before he was blown up by the IRA. When the new terminal building was opened by HRH Prince Phillip on 11 December 1972, Eddie was able to spend a considerable amount of time with him. He also concluded from his meetings that Prince Charles would make a fine king – we still wait to find out! The protocol in those days for royal visits was for the Lord Lieutenant for the area of the royal visit (usually Cardiff or Glamorgan) to greet the visitor on the apron as they deplaned, often accompanied by the chairman of the local council involved with the visit.

Eddie's celebrity list continues with four Prime Ministers (Harold Wilson, Edward Heath, Jim Callaghan and Margaret Thatcher), seven Secretaries of State for Wales, including George Thomas, and a whole raft of politicians such as Roy Jenkins, Michael Heseltine, Jeremy Thorpe, Tony Benn ('a very pleasant man'), George Brown and Dennis Healey ('he likes a drink'). But apart from his meeting with Henry Kissinger, probably the most significant VIP to use Rhoose and whom Eddie was able to welcome, on Wednesday 2 June 1982, was Pope John Paul II, as part of his five-day pastoral visit to Britain (see Chapter 11).

Glamair were a charter, air taxi and flight-training company founded by Bernard Haddican at Rhoose in 1973 with a Piper PA-34 Seneca G-AZVJ; the company had been trading before this as Bernell Aviation, operating the Cardiff/Wales Flying Club, initially with Grumman AA-5 Travellers, and operating from one of the airport's old wartime Nashcrete buildings on the airport's south side and close to the old terminal building. Kraken-Air was another of the early Rhoose-based air taxi companies, an offshoot of the Kraken Engineering Co. from Swansea, who also used Piper PA-23 Aztec aircraft.

Based at Cardiff for many years with a series of different executive aircraft was Dovey Holdings, their aircraft identified by the red/black flag on their tail with a 'D' in its centre – they were the forerunner of what is now called fractional ownership: the aircraft were available for charter and use by several local companies, as well as Dovey themselves. They were founded by Len Dovey, whose Cardiff-based companies included Dovey Motors. Dovey's Piper Aztecs G-BGBS and G-HARV were initially used for inter-group transport, but began to operate in 1980 as Cardiff Air Taxi Services, with a base at Bristol Lulsgate as well. Terry Fox, ex-Air Wales, became Dovey's operations manager, with Cessna 421 Golden Eagle (G-BAEI) joining their fleet, flown by company pilot Geoff 'Curley' Wadhams on its frequent business flights to Cork. Other aircraft operated by Dovey included a Cessna 414 (G-BTSG), a Beech Duke (G-DHLD), a Beech King Air 90 (EI-BHL) and a Cessna 550 Citation executive jet VP-CLD, disposed of in 2007. The current incumbent for executive and corporate travel options based at Rhoose is Dragon Fly – Executive Air Charter with a pair of Beechcraft 200 Super King Airs G-BVMA and G-MEGN.

A short-lived air taxi operation Air Ladvale moved in at Rhoose in December 1978 from its initial base at Gloucester/Staverton where they operated three seven-seat aircraft. Derek Phillips from Caerleon, whose flying career at Rhoose had started with the Glamorgan Flying Club, headed up Air Ladvale at Rhoose, using a Beagle 206 for ad hoc charters and air taxi work. The company quoted a figure of £620 as the cost of carrying seven passengers to Paris and back – business was not brisk and by spring of 1979 the company had disappeared.

In 1980 RB Aviation Ltd was formed, operating as Cambrian Air at Rhoose and Executive Air at Gloucester's Staverton Airport, flying a Piper Navajo Chieftain, Aztec and Seneca for air taxi work. RB was also associated with the flying training of the Cambrian Flying Club. They attempted, unsuccessfully, to launch a north–south Welsh air link following the demise of Air Wales in its first incarnation (see Chapter 5).

From the 1980s another resident Rhoose aviation company developed, Veritair, established by Julian Verity, as a helicopter charter company with initially a single Bell B206 Jet Ranger. For a while the company branched out into fixed-wing charter work, using King Air G-BIXM. With the opening of the Cardiff Heliport at Tremorfa (just a stone's throw from the site of Cardiff's airport at Pengam Moors), Veritair moved out from Rhoose. Veritair, now part of the British International Group, also operate Cardiff Heliport.

South Wales' industrial concerns continue to attract a huge variety of business jets to the airport. For the official opening of the new Bosch factory at Miskin on 25 September 1991 visiting business jets carrying officials for the event included the trio of BAe125s, HB-VGF and 'G plus D-CMIR. When the Sony factory at Pencoed was opened by Diana, Princess of Wales on 14 September 1993 Sony officials flew to Rhoose in their corporate Falcons N70TH and N71TH.

Rhoose's association with flight training probably started in the mid-1960s with Rhoose becoming a popular destination for the operators of training aircraft, notably multi-engine trainers. First amongst these must be the Hamble-based College of Air Training, the BOAC/BEA subsidiary that provided flying scholarships to potential commercial pilots for the nation's national airlines. *Ab initio* training flights were flown at Hamble in the college's DHC-1 Chipmunks, but, having qualified, the students spread their wings using a fleet of Piper PA-23 Apache twins. These were frequent visitors to Rhoose and to the skies above South Wales – on clear winter's nights the skies were often alive with flashing lights on College Apaches practising instrument flight, tracking from the Ibsley VOR (Hampshire) to the Brecon VOR and then to the Compton VOR. After Hamble was closed considerable pilot training was undertaken by CSE Aviation from Oxford and their Piper PA-34 Senecas and PA-28s used Rhoose on many hundreds of occasions. Rhoose is still a popular destination for such flights by Airways Flight Training (Beech Duchess from Exeter and Bournemouth), Oxford Aviation Academy (Piper Seneca from Oxford) and CTC Aviation (Diamond DA-42 Twin Star from Bournemouth), and rarely a day goes by without an inbound training flight by one of these companies, usually so that the trainee pilot can practise an ILS approach, flying off at a decision height on short finals and not actually landing. Even RAF aircraft, particularly C-130s, practise ILS approaches at Rhoose.

10

CLUB FLYING

Cardiff Aeroplane Club were founded at Pengam Moors aerodrome in 1931, a very active and dynamic club where students could learn to fly – some were part of a government subsidy scheme which in 1934 paid £25 to the club for each new pilot trained – and as a focus for private owners and light aircraft (what today is known as general aviation or GA) operations. Pre-war, eight London-Cardiff air races were held, the last on 10 September 1938, culminating at Pengam. With the war, Cardiff Aeroplane Club closed, but its post-war successor Glamorgan Flying Club at Rhoose can be directly traced back to these pre-war roots. Although civil commercial flying ceased at Pengam in 1954, Cardiff Aeroplane Club held out there until the airfield finally died in 1958.

Prior to this, around 1956, some former members of the Cardiff Aeroplane Club established Glamorgan Aviation, a limited company with a registered office at Quay Street Chambers in Cardiff and with the primary aim of forming a flying club at Rhoose. Using the former wartime Nashcrete guardroom at the airport's former main entrance – just to the east and on the Barry side of the current fire station – Glamorgan Flying Club commenced operations at Rhoose at the end of 1956. Initially they operated Tiger Moth G-AOUY, soon adding Austers G-AGVN and G-ANHX. Post-war there were government restrictions on the import of foreign light aircraft to the UK, so the opportunities to buy the 'fancy new' US trainers being built by Cessna and Piper eluded the Glamorgan Flying Club; and in any case war-surplus Austers and Tiger Moths were much cheaper to acquire. Later came the Thruxton Jackaroo (a converted Tiger Moth with enclosed cockpit) G-APJV and two Percival Prentices G-AOPL and G-AOLP, which were actually owned by club members.

Glamorgan Flying Club immediately hit the GA headlines in 1958 when they hosted the third Popular Flying Association (PFA) rally or fly-in at Rhoose – the second PFA rally had been held at Sywell, Northants, in 1957. The PFA was formed from the earlier post-war ULAA (Ultra-Light Aircraft Association, founded in 1946) in 1952. The PFA support the home building of light aircraft in the UK and issued permits to fly on behalf of the Civil Aviation Authority. The PFA changed their name to the LAA (Light Aircraft Association) in 2008 but still perform the same function for a fleet that now numbers over 2,000 light aircraft. Back in 1958 there were very few home-builts, and, as it always has, the PFA also embraced those pilots and their aircraft whose spirit was to fly for fun. The weekend of 14 and 15 June 1958 was fine and dry, and with Glamorgan Aviation as hosts and organisers, the words of the editorial of the July/August 1958 edition of the PFA's magazine, *Popular Flying*, neatly summarise the successful Rhoose event:

Seven French aircraft and about thirty British aircraft turned up at Rhoose, the French contingent slightly late, having added inadvertently to the items of another display when, delayed by weather, they stopped at Elstree for lunch. A first-class bar was waiting for crews after they had booked in and Glamorgan Aviation had organised a cold meal in a large marquee. As one sat in the shade of the tent, scoffing one's cold ham and looking out at the rows of light aircraft parked in the brilliant sunshine, while others droned peacefully overhead, it was evident that light aviation was not dead yet – not by a long chalk!

In the evening the rally participants moved to the Angel Hotel in Cardiff for the rally's presentation dinner. A fly-in by thirty-seven aircraft may not seem that noteworthy, but by 1958 standards, when light aviation and GA were struggling to establish sport flying in the UK after the depravities of the war, this event at Rhoose was probably one of the largest post-war gatherings of light aircraft anywhere in Europe.

Denys Martin, Roy Brown and their committee were the main organisers for the event at Rhoose. Other founder members of the ULAA and PFA such as Arthur W.J.G. Ord-Hume were also responsible for invitations to the 'French contingent' from the sister organisation to the PFA in France, the *Réseau du Sport de l'Air* (RSA). The RSA's president Georges Béraud flew to Rhoose in his Jodel/CEA DR.1050 Ambassadeur F-BJJL to support the PFA in its endeavours, a gesture of major significance. Some of the other participating aircraft were:

F-BIAY	Piel 301 Emeraude	M. Vieux
F-BIMG	Coopavia 301 Emeraude	Francis Cousenon
F-PEVM	Jodel D.112	
F-PHUC	Gardan Minicab	Jean Barritault
F-PHZH	Jodel D119	
F-PJKA	Barritault JB-1 Minicab	Jean Barritault
F-BJJL	CEA/Jodel DR1050	Georges Béraud
G-ABTC	Comper Swift	Tony Cole
G-AEMW	BA Swallow II	Swallow Flying Group
G-AESE	DH.87B Hornet Moth	
G-AFJR	Tipsy B	
G-AHVS	Taylorcraft Plus D	Neville Birch
G-AHVU	DH.82A Tiger Moth	Chris Roberts
G-AISA	Tipsy Trainer B1	
G-AJOZ	Fairchild 24W Argus 2	Barry Birch
G-AKFN	Fairchild 24W Argus	Mr Allchin
G-A???	Miles Gemini	A.J. Linnell
G-AOTJ	Auster 5	A.J. Pezner
G-APIZ	Rollason D31 Turbulent	Joan Short

In the PFA's magazine prior to the event pilots were given advice on arrival procedures – one of these is '… recently two television masts have been erected rather closer to the field than we would have liked. One at Wenvoe and the other at St. Hilary …' Other landmarks were pointed out: '… Rhoose is easy to find. The first two markers are the cement works chimney of the Aberthaw Cement Company which lies almost due south of the airfield, the other, which carries four chimneys, lying to the west. Beyond this is the town of Barry with its large dock area …' Pilots were also warned of the proximity of Llandow (which was disused) and St Athan, described as 'a very large RAF station whose main runway is over 5000ft long'.

Arthur W.J.G. Ord-Hume, who was one of the six founder members of the ULAA, was at this 1958 event; his photos, taken on a 1926 Eastman-Kodak 116-size box camera, are used as the illustrations in this book.

Jean Barritault flying his Minicab F-PJKA along the South Wales coast during the 1958 PFA rally somewhere west of Rhoose, probably near the Leys or Aberthaw. (Arthur W. Ord-Hume)

With his Jodel DR1050, the President of France's *Réseau du Sport de l'Air* (RSA), Georges Béraud was an inspirational visitor to the 1958 PFA Rally at Rhoose. (Arthur W. Ord-Hume)

Lines of aircraft on the grass to the west of the control tower at the end of the 3 June 1960 London–Cardiff Air Race. (LMLHS)

Built on premises at Rhoose between 1960–64 by members of the Cardiff Ultralight Aeroplane Club, this homebuilt Piel CP.301 Emeraude G-ARUV is seen with Peter Harrison soon after its first flight in 1964. (Geoff Jones)

The PFA rally at Rhoose was a memorable occasion if only for the dreadful state of the landing area (many of these light aircraft landed on the grass in an area between the thresholds of runways 22 and 31). As I recall it the airfield appeared to have been abandoned for many years and had partly succumbed to Nature. It was on this occasion that French pilot Jean Barritault and I finalised arrangements over the Gardan Minicab design, and afterwards I bought the remains of the old business. Yes, Minicab F-PHUC was at Rhoose and poor Jean could not understand why we ex-RAF types all pointed to the registration letters on the side of his aeroplane and roared with laughter. Alternative pronunciations of consonantal verbs are hard to convey across languages!

It is often forgotten that Rhoose had a third, grass runway 08/26 which ran through the intersection of the two hard runways and was frequently used by light aircraft and very occasionally by Dakotas of Cambrian Airways and other airlines when there was a very strong westerly wind. On one occasion in the early 1960s a Slingsby Skylark glider arrived over Rhoose one afternoon, having flown from the Derbyshire Gliding Club site at Great Hucklow – non-radio, the pilot let down on the dead side, joined the circuit and landed on the grass. All perfectly legal in those days!

Another club that moved from Pengam to Rhoose was the Cardiff Ultralight Aeroplane Club, bringing with them the Tipsy Trainer 1 G-AISA, and in an amicable arrangement they shared Glamorgan Flying Club's premises. They swapped the Tipsy for a French Jodel D.117 G-ARYW (ex-F-BIBS) in May 1962, but this change ended in tragedy on the evening of 16 August 1962 when shortly after taking off from Rhoose the Jodel crashed, killing the instructor Ivor Lewis and his student Malcolm Fox. The club continued to operate with Bill O'Neil as its instructor, acquiring the Fairtravel Linnet G-APRH, which they operated for several years until this club faded away. Some of its members joined the growing ranks of aircraft homebuilders, and in a building close to the old fire station (near to where the current terminal stands) built a French-designed wood and fabric two-seater, the Piel CP.301 Emeraude G-ARUV; with a Continental C-90-14F engine, this aircraft was first test flown at Rhoose on 27 July 1963 by Alan Wakefield for its builder Peter Harrison, an executive at the time with Tarmac Construction. It left Rhoose when Peter Harrison relocated to Blackpool and forty-seven years later the aircraft is still airworthy, flying from Keevil in Gloucestershire.

Bob Thursby casts his memory back to Glamorgan Flying Club in the late 1950s:

> The first instructors were George Kemp, late of the Cardiff Aeroplane Club and a chap called Paul Cash who I never got to meet. The clubhouse was established in the former guardroom, by then vacated by the police. Later Chief Flying Instructors were Vernon Bernard, J.A. 'Ben' Bennett and Sid 'Smithy' Smith. I learnt to fly with the Glamorgan Flying Club in these early years and later had the dubious distinction of being the last pilot to fly under the Glamorgan Aviation banner when in November 1962 I taxied Auster G-AGVN in to the hands of the receivers!

One of Glamorgan Aviations lasting legacies at Rhoose was their construction of a small hangar to the south-west of Cambrian's maintenance hangar; here they employed a full-time engineer to carry out light aircraft maintenance. When Glamorgan Aviation failed, this hangar was taken over by Cambrian Airways to house their pilot link-training unit.

The 1958 PFA rally set the ball rolling and in 1959, 1960 and 1961 Rhoose was the focus for the London to Cardiff air races, again organised at Rhoose by the enthusiastic members of the Glamorgan Flying Club. This was a revival of pre-war London to Cardiff air races held in the 1930s and which terminated at Pengam Moors. The first post-war air race event was on Saturday 13 June 1959, billed as the 'Welsh International Air Rally' in the event brochure and in which Roy Brown, the chairman of Glamorgan Aviation Ltd, said:

> Cardiff (Rhoose) Airport, fully equipped with the most modern aids, has been developed as a result of the dedicated effort of many people as a capital city airport. As such it offers comprehensive and comfortable airline travel, charter, flying training, pleasure flying, aircraft hire and social facilities,

and it is our hope that through today's event you will be encouraged to make increasing use of the airfield in the future.

There was free admission to the public and with the arrivals of visiting aircraft from 1000hrs onwards, the flying display programme started at 1500hrs, including the Welsh Air Rally Race. Music during the afternoon was played by the No.557 (Pontypridd Grammar School) Squadron Military Band under the direction of Flg Off. H.G. Davies. Sixteen different prizes were up for grabs for participating pilots, ranging from the premier *Western Mail-Welsh Air Rally Trophy* to six pairs of nylon stockings for the first lady pilot to arrive at the rally, donated by Max Harris Esq. of Cardiff. The brochure contained a range of contemporary advertising: John Morgan, The Hayes, Cardiff, had a full-page advert proclaiming that they had supplied 'the clubhouse curtains'. Stirling Moss sent his best wishes on behalf of BP, and there were adverts from Jackaroo Aircraft Ltd, makers of the Thruxton Jackaroo biplane and Aviation Traders, who had supplied two of their civilianised Percival Prentice aircraft to members of the club. Two thousand pounds would buy you a Prentice with a three-year Certificate of Airworthiness and for an additional £200 they would fit long-range fuel and oil tanks, according to the advert.

Glyn Rees, proprietor of East Glam Motors, a bus and coach operator based at Nelson, and future owner of Glamorgan Flying Club, participated in the significantly more ambitious 3 and 4 June 1960 International Welsh Air Rally. The highlight was the Friday 3 June London to Cardiff Air Race, in which Glyn Rees was flying the Percival Prentice G-AOPL, part of an extremely large field of forty-one aircraft who, with staggered and handicapped starting times based on their declared speeds, took off from White Waltham (west of London) starting at 1700hrs. The Claude Grahame-White Challenge Cup was the main trophy being competed for, plus £100 cash, and it was won by John Stewart-Wood at 134.25mph, piloting his Auster 5 G-AIKE. The pilots participating read like a 'who's who' from light aviation of the era: Peter Masefield, Percy Blamire, Ernie Crabtree, Charles Boddington, Viv Bellamy, Norman 'N.H.' Jones, Sheila Scott, Gillian Cazalet, plus the locals Glyn Rees and Cliff Hubbard (Prentice G-AOLP), and aircraft that ranged from the Spitfire Mk VIII G-AIDN to six diminutive, single-seat, VW-powered Rollason D.31 Turbulents, all from the Tiger Club, and three flown by Joan Short (G-APIZ), Margo McKellar (G-APBZ) and Norman Jones (G-APVZ). The air race itinerary for the 1960 event also included the Saturday morning races, Class I, II and III National Air Races – Short Circuit for the Air League Challenge Cup, Norton-Griffiths Challenge Trophy and de Havilland Tiger Moth Challenge Trophy, each with a £30 cash prize. The winners of these races were respectively: Dennis Hartas flying Jodel D117 G-APOZ, John Stewart-Wood flying Auster 5 G-AIKE and joint winners, both flying Thruxton Jackaroos, Sheila Scott flying G-APAM and Geoffrey Marler flying G-APAP. After the races the pilots and guests retired to the marquee for the President's Luncheon, conducted in two sittings because of the numbers. From 1400hrs until 1700hrs there was a 'flying programme', the highlight of which was the formation aerobatic display by the Hawker Hunter jets of No.111 Squadron RAF, the Black Arrows – four Hunting Jet Provosts from the Central Flying School at RAF Little Rissington also flew in, XM355, '57, '60 and '61. The 1730hrs prize giving was by the president and Mrs John Morgan. The event programme was again a pot pourri of contemporary advertising, including Cambrian Airways and Derby Airways, who were offering direct air services from Rhoose to the Costa Brava, Luxembourg, Majorca and Ostend with the strap line, Save A Day – Fly D.A. Glamorgan Aviation Ltd were also offering pleasure flights, 15s for adults and 10s for children.

The 1961 International Welsh Air Rally was held on 2 and 3 June, again with the London to Cardiff air race the highlight, being the opening race of the 1961 National Air Races and flown this year from Panshangar (north of London) to Rhoose. It was a royal occasion with a fleeting visit from HRH the Duke of Edinburgh, who had entered a Turbulent in the race; he arrived in Cardiff by train and was driven to Rhoose, arriving at 1700hrs but at 1800hrs left by air in a DH.114 Heron of the Queen's Flight (XH375) for London. The eclectic race line up of thirty-three entrants for the 114-nautical-mile course on the Friday afternoon and evening race included two Spitfires and eight Tiger Moths. The biggest disappointment was the non-appearance of Ron Flockhart's P-51 Mustang G-ARKD because it had become 'stranded' in Athens, Greece. For the first time modern US-built light singles were competing, G-ARAA, a Cessna 182 flown by Wing Commander R.H. McIntosh, and G-ARAT, a Cessna 180 flown by L. Richards. HRH the Duke of Edinburgh's entrant in the single-seat Rollason D.31 Turbulent G-APNZ was Wing Commander J. de Milt Severne who came twenty-seventh out of forty. The winner of the London to Cardiff race at a speed of 318mph was Viv Bellamy flying his Spitfire Mk VIII G-AIDN, for which he was awarded the new John Morgan Air Racing Challenge Trophy. The programme for Saturday 3 June was similar to 1960's. Glyn Rees had flown the Tiger Moth G-AOUY in the London to Cardiff air race and qualified for the 15 July King's Cup Air Race at Bagington as a result; his co-pilot was the young aspiring pilot Neil Williams. During the 1961 event at Rhoose the pilots competed for the three other trophies in various classes, although the cash prizes had reduced to £25 for the winner of each, and Glyn Rees flying 'UY won the de Havilland Tiger Moth Trophy, flying three laps of the 11.6-mile circuit at an average speed of 106.5mph. Most notable was the large-scale appearance of the first US-built 'spam-cans', Cessnas, Pipers, etc., and a Forney Aircoupe G-ARHA. The Piper Apache G-APCL, plus Cessna 310 G-ARCI, and the second British-owned Cessna 175A G-APZS and a Cessna 180 G-ARAT heralded the start of the demise of Britain's light aircraft industry with the flood of cheaper, more efficient imports from the US, a situation that still prevails fifty years later. Nonetheless, the stalwarts of British sport flying were still at Rhoose, including many Tiger Moths, a Thruxton Jackaroo, Proctors, a Miles M.18 G-AHKY, Comper Swift G-ABUS and Arrow Active G-ABVE. But 1961 was the end of a never to be repeated era at Rhoose. Sadly, the various trophies connected with these events, including the prestigious London to Cardiff Air Race trophy, one of which dated from pre-war days and was kept on club premises, were stolen in a burglary some years later.

With all clubs there is inevitable member discord, and Glamorgan was no exception. A new Rhoose Flying Club was formed, occupying a wooden building on the north side of the airport and starting flying operations with an Auster 5 G-ANFU loaned from Stan Stennett. This was complemented by a Tiger Moth and later still by a Cessna 172. Stan Stennett, the well-known Welsh entertainer and star of the *Black and White Minstrel Show*, owned a succession of interesting aircraft that were based at Rhoose, including a tail-dragger Cessna 170 converted to nose-wheel configuration (G-APVS), the V-tail Bonanza G-APTY 'The Minstrel' and the Cessna 310 twin G-ATCR. Through many changes the Rhoose Flying Club ended up as the Pegasus Flying Club.

Pilot Margo McKellar shows a leg climbing out of her Tiger Club Rollason Turbulent G-APBZ during the 1960 Welsh Air Rally. (LMLHS)

Above Arrow Active Mk.II G-ABVE was an unusual participant in the 1960 London–Cardiff Air Race. The former airport fire station building can be seen in the background. (Colin Dodds)

Left Moth Minor G-AFOZ and Tiger Moth G-ANZZ round a pylon during the three laps of the 4 June Norton Griffiths Challenge Trophy race in the 1960 Welsh Air Rally. (LMLHS)

Sheila Scott, flying her Thruxton Jackaroo G-APAM *Myth*, was placed fourth in the 1960 London-Cardiff air race. Later in the weekend she was first in the Class 3 race at 104mph – here she receives her trophy for this win, the first of an extensive list of race wins she achieved during the 1960s. (LMLHS)

Glamorgan Flying Club President John Morgan, pictured in 1960. He was also Chairman of Cambrian Airways from July 1958 to May 1967. (LMLHS)

Spitfire Tr.8 G-AIDN won the 1961 London–Cardiff Air Race, and also flew in the 1960 event, both times piloted by Viv Bellamy. (Colin Dodds)

Some of the 1961 Welsh Air Rally participants: G-APJV Thruxton Jackaroo, a Tiger Moth, Auster, Proctor and Anson. (Colin Dodds)

A 1961 air race participant entered by the Hampshire Aeroplane Club, a Currie Wot G-APWT. (Colin Dodds)

Welsh entertainer and TV star Stan Stennett, a keen private aviator at Rhoose, owned many different light aircraft, his most well known during the 1960s being the 'V-tail' Beech Bonanza G-APTY, named *The Minstrel*. (Mike Kemp Collection)

Meanwhile, the members of the Glamorgan Flying Club met and decided to form another club and, as Glamorgan Aviation was now defunct, started as Glamorgan Flying Club Ltd. Initially this was begun with the Auster G-AHSW, which Glamorgan Aviation had purchased some years before, an aircraft that had started life with the Cardiff Aeroplane Club at Pengam in about 1948. Club chairman was John Morgan, also chairman of Cambrian Airways, Cambrian's operations manager B.J.T. 'Jim' Callan took over from him. Some of the other members of the club at this time included Colin Davies, an agricultural merchants rep; Illtyd Jones; John Griffiths; J.A. 'Ben' Bennett, an ex-RAF Spitfire pilot who left to join the College of Air Training at Hamble; Sid 'Smithy' Smith; and A.J. 'Tony' Miles, then a grocer in Barry who subsequently joined Cambrian Airways as a pilot and ended up as a Boeing 747 captain with British Airways. A Piper Tripacer G-ARAX was also in the Glamorgan Flying Club fleet in the early 1960s and the Auster G-AHSW was exchanged for a new Auster J5F Aiglet Trainer G-AMTB, which Bob Thursby describes as 'the nicest aeroplane I've flown, although the pilot had to consider the oil content before the fuel'. Once again around 1964–65 this club got in to financial difficulties and the majority shareholding was given to Glyn Rees, who became de facto owner/manager of Glamorgan Flying Club for many years – he put John Keith Pickett, owner of the DH.85 Leopard Moth G-ATFU, in place to manage the new club. In 1965 Glyn disposed of the Auster and bought the French-designed Jodel DR1051 G-ASRP. They also had use of one of the early Cessna 172s to be imported to the UK from the USA, registered G-ARCM, and, in fact, owned by Billy Butlin's son-in-law – it was later sold to a club member, Bill Griffiths. In 1964 they were the first club in the UK to acquire the Australian-designed and built Victa Airtourer, the first two at Rhoose being G-ASYZ and 'ZA. Glosair at Staverton were the UK agents, assembling these aerobatic, all-metal two-seaters from kits that were containerised for delivery to Staverton. The club's Airtourer 'ZA came to grief in spectacular manner during a forced landing on a playing field in Caerphilly on 26 May 1966, when due to vibrations in the stick, the instructor, one Bob Cole, feared the tail was about to detach – it was only the rubber mat wing walk on the top of the wing next to the cockpit which had become partially detached and was flapping violently and disturbing the air flow over the tail. Fortunately, both occupants walked away uninjured after this landing. Glosair made significant changes to the original Airtourer design and the type was redesignated the Glosairtourer 115 – Glamorgan FC acquired a succession of these popular aircraft, two of them still surviving at Rhoose, G-AZOF, owned and flown by Bob Thursby, and G-AWMI, awaiting some care in the old Robin hangar next to Aeros and the Rhoose Flying Club cafe.

Glamorgan Flying Club also had a Piper Caribbean G-ARHN on strength in the mid-1960s. By the early 1970s they had a fleet of Airtourers, Grumman AA-1 and AA-5 aircraft and at least one Cessna 172, with some of the Grummans detached on lease to a club at Swansea. Dick Smerdon, a very experienced ex-Second World War pilot, became the club's CFI until he left to found the flying club at Bodmin. Jersey resident Bernard Haddican was then the owner of the club, a well-known businessman who had made his money in the building trade. As well as interests at Rhoose, he also had aviation interests in the Channel Islands and at Exeter, and he was involved with Intra Airways, which later became JEA and flybe. He also owned the Dragon Rapide G-ASGH, which was based at Rhoose for a while and was proudly wheeled on to the main apron in October 1979 when the first Concorde visited Rhoose. This aircraft was later sold to Phillip Meeson, founder and owner of Channel Express and Jet2. It was at Exeter that Glamorgan Flying Club's aircraft were then maintained under Haddican's reign. In summer 1978 Glamorgan lost the lucrative RAF flying scholarship contract it had won, one of the instructors, John Morgan, left and the remaining staff pulled together and rented two Cessna 150s from 'flying vet' Maurice Kirk to remain operational, the Airtourers and Cherokees being disposed of.

Another club formed at Rhoose was the South Wales Flying Club in 1969, founded by the Second World War Typhoon, Tempest ace and high-scoring V-1 killer Bob Cole. It welcomed a tall, thin CFI from recent flying jobs at Land's End and in Kenya to teach students in the

Used by the Glamorgan Flying Club during 1964–65, the Cessna 172B G-ARCM. (Geoff Jones)

Glamorgan Flying Club was the first in the UK to buy Victa Airtourer G-ASZA, seen in 1964 on the grass next to the club and close to the runway 31 threshold. (Geoff Jones)

South Wales Flying Club used this Bolkow Junior G-ATUI from mid-1969 onwards. (Geoff Jones)

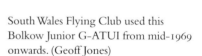

With Welsh pilots in the team, the Rothmans-sponsored Rothmans Aerobatic team and their Pitts S.2 Specials visited Rhoose on several occasions, such as on 19 April 1979. (Kelvin Lumb)

club's Bolkow Bo208c Junior G-ATUI – they later acquired a Cherokee 140. This CFI was Chris Unitt, brought up across the water near Filton aerodrome and who had been flying Super Cubs and Dragon Rapides in Kenya and Dragon Rapides and Austers at Land's End. Chris describes the Bolkow as one of the aeroplane exceptions: 'Most aircraft that look right fly well, and those that are ugly don't – the Bolkow Junior confounded this theory and whilst not a "looker", it flew superbly, even though its cockpit was rather small. It could perform basic aerobatics extremely well.' Chris and the South Wales Flying Club operated from a small room in a wooden hut on the south side, furnished meagrely with a desk, filing cabinet and old-fashioned, black-buttoned 'A' and 'B'-type pay phone as contact to the outside world. He stayed instructing at Rhoose, building valuable flying hours, for two years before moving on to a career in commercial flying with Guernsey Airlines/Alidair, Aurigny Air Services and, his last job before retirement in 2010, flying DHC-8-400s with flybe. Chris was replaced by Capt. Arthur Miller, an ex-RAF and KLM DC-8 pilot, who introduced some innovative ideas for getting increased utilisation out of the club aircraft, but he left in early 1973 and both S. Wales and Pegasus relocated to one of the Nashcrete buildings, merged under the Pegasus name and got a new CFI, Bob Jones, an ex-RAF flying instructor and transport pilot who had recently returned from teaching Saudi pilots on BAC Strikemaster jets.

In 1981 Cambrian Flying Club were going strong with stalwarts Barry Mahoney and Mike Mylan as instructors operating the two PA-38 Tomahawks G-BGZJ and G-BGSS, plus PA-28 Warrior G-BGVK. Two other Tomahawks G-BGZF and G-BGXB, plus a Cessna 182 and Piper Seneca G-EXEC, were all disposed of during the year. However, the Club's 'Superclub', operating around a Cessna 172 Hawk XP G-BFIF, continued to be popular amongst its members. Over the weekend of 4–6 September 1981 the club, plus many members in their own aircraft, made a visit to the Aero Club Loire-Atlantique at Nantes in western France. Cardiff is twinned with Nantes and it was felt that liaison between the flying clubs of the two cities would be appropriate. Eight aircraft made it from Rhoose to Nantes, including Nigel Calder (despite forgetting to bring his passport) in his Cessna 172 G-BIRO and John Powell in his piston Provost G-BGSB/WV494, an interesting Rhoose resident at the time.

Around 1979 the Rothmans Aerobatic team took up temporary residence at Rhoose, having moved in from their previous base at Teesside when Bridgend pilot Marcus Edwards was the leader, just as the team were winding down after a successful decade of air show appearances, first with four Stampe biplanes and then with Pitts S-2As. Local aviation hero Neil Williams also flew with the Rothmans team until his untimely death in 1977 whilst ferrying a Spanish-built Heinkel back to the UK. When the Rothmans sponsorship ended Marcus Edwards formed the VIXEN TWO team at Rhoose, using his ex-Rothmans Pitts G-BDKS, with RAF Coastal Command pilot John McClean flying Pitts G-BECM. John would frequently fly up to Rhoose from his home in Cornwall to train with Marcus and pick up their aircraft, which

Some of the Piper Tomahawks and Cessna 150s used by the flying club at Rhoose in 1981. (Geoff Jones)

With the 1979 Rhoose Carnival Queen and her Maid of Honour in attendance, students of the Cambrian Aviation Centre receive their Private Pilot Licence certificates in an informal ceremony. From left to right: Lawrence Russell, Graham Court, John Williams, Les Nation, ?, the author Geoff Jones, Jimmy James. (Geoff Jones)

One of the Robin hangar's long-term residents, Geoff Claxton's Jodel D.112 G-ASXY which sadly crashed near Swansea on 13 March 2011, killing Geoff, a life-long grass roots aviation enthusiast and pilot. (Geoff Jones)

were maintained at Rhoose by Bob Lea. Andy Wallbridge with Pitts G-BADY joined them to make a three-ship formation team, but unfortunately in 1984, whilst performing at Fleetwood, Lancashire, John and Andy were involved in a mid-air collision and both were killed. The John McClean Aerobatic Trophy was named in his honour. Marcus became involved with the Snowbird microlight that was built at Llandow. In the 1990s Marcus became involved with de Havilland Aviation as their chief pilot, the brainchild of another Rhoose pilot, Gwyn Jones, who had learnt to fly at the Pegasus Flying Club and had kept his Harvard G-BDAM at the airport for some time. De Havilland set up at Swansea Airport to restore and maintain DH Vampires and a Sea Vixen in flying condition for air-display purposes. There was serious talk of moving the operation to Rhoose, but unexpectedly Marcus Edwards died and the whole enterprise was moved to Bournemouth.

A Rhoose institution for decades, the Glamorgan Flying Club disappeared when it was sold to RB Aviation Ltd of Swindon in 1979, renamed the Cambrian Flying Club (known as the Cambrian Aviation Centre), with Cliff Hubbard as the CFI. With the RAF contract restarting, to provide ten hours' of *ab initio* training to prospective new pilots, they embarked on an impressive re-equipment programme with a fleet of Piper PA-38 Tomahawks and a

Piper Warrior. Based in one of the Nashcrete buildings alongside the former south-side main apron, Cambrian Flying Club shared the accommodation with Executive Express, who were flying night-time Datapost and other charters (see Chapter 6). However, financial difficulties loomed, Cliff Hubbard left and one of the instructors, Barry Mahoney, reorganised the business sufficiently to enable it to be sold to Tony Clemo (see Chapter 5). It then passed through the hands of several owners, Mike Mylan in 1984 to Niall McGarry and then Dave Jones, who, with competition from the newly formed Cardiff Wales Flying Club, changed the club's name back to Glamorgan Flying Club. Various characters came and went at this club, but its operations soon fizzled out. In 1981 following an approach to the Cambrian Flying Club from Phil Lewis, a QFI (Qualified Flying Instructor) from Swansea, the Cambrian Flying Club (Swansea) was established, which after ownership changes and a move to Pembrey for a while, is still operating at Swansea thirty-one years on.

Cardiff Wales Flying Club was established by disaffected members of a group within the Cambrian Flying Club, the 'Superclub' who had leased a Cessna 172 G-BFGD for their members. Prime movers in this new club were Dave Howell, Steve Mathews and the well-known BBC Radio Wales broadcaster of the time, Mike Flynn, who acquired a Piper PA-38 Tomahawk with which to commence flight training. When Steve Mathews left several others stepped into the CFI role for short periods of time, Nigel Hughes from Pontypridd, ex-RAF and Cambrian Airways pilot Peter Williams and, last but not least, Terry Blockley. Despite several changes and competition from other clubs, Cardiff Wales Flying Club soldiered on into the late 1990s, first under the management of Manx Airlines pilot Dave Sarver and finally under Chris Good.

Cardiff Aero Flying School was set up in 1991 with renegade from the Cardiff Wales Flying Club Terry Blockley as the CFI and Sue Jenkins, who had learnt to fly with the earlier Cardiff Wales Flying Club and owned a Cessna 172 and Slingsby Firefly, as a director. This club ran out of steam by 1990 and Terry Blockley left to fly with Len Dovey.

The Cardiff Academy of Aviation began operations from the 'white house' in 2003, providing flight training and aircraft hire with a Tomahawk, Robin R2210 and Piper Warrior. Chris Good was the CFI but the organisation was sold on to one of the academy's instructors, who couldn't juggle flying commercially for charter company Dragonfly with operating the flight training company, and the latter faltered and closed.

Unfortunately, around 2000 the airport authorities decided that all international general aviation flights from and to Rhoose should be handled by a resident handling company. Prior to this customs and special branch clearance (for those aircraft from and to the Channel Islands, Isle of Man and Ireland, areas subject to the Prevention of Terrorism Act) had been freely available to pilots. Now Signature would organise this, but at a cost that only the wealthiest of pilots could afford – the frequent gaggle of light aircraft often seen on stand 1 and, before that, in the 1970s, 1980s and 1990s, on stand 13, dried up. UK-originating general aviation aircraft, not requiring customs, special branch or flight plans could use the club apron on the south side. When the flying and flight training club folded at the end of 2008 there was no practical access for visiting light aircraft at Rhoose. Fortunately, with the June 2010 arrival of Aeros, they took on responsibility for escorting pilots air-side and collecting the appropriate landing and parking fees, but still not for aircraft requiring customs or special branch clearance. In late 2010 Signature moved their operation to the south side, in the 'white house' next to Aeros, and the welcome mat again appeared to be out for general aviation aircraft of all shapes and sizes and at reasonable prices.

In an almost unprecedented move on 11 June 2011, the airport hosted a Jodel fly-in in memory of Geoff Claxton, who had based his Jodel D.112 G-ASXY at Rhoose for many years and was tragically killed on 13 March of that year whilst making a forced landing near Swansea on a flight in his Jodel from Rhoose to Haverfordwest. The flying club hosted a barbecue and all proceeds went to the Wales Air Ambulance.

11

DIVERSITY

Many members of the royal family have used Rhoose Airport during official visits to South Wales. The Queen has visited on several occasions, the first in January 1969 (see Chapter 9). Although Pope John Paul II arrived in Great Britain at Gatwick Airport on an Alitalia aircraft on 28 May 1982, it was a British Caledonian BAC1-11 (G-BJRT) used for his six-day pastoral tour of England, Scotland and Wales. On the morning of Wednesday 2 June the pontiff's BAC1-11 arrived from Edinburgh and touched down at Rhoose, where a huge crowd had gathered to greet him. John Paul II descended the aircraft steps and, having given his customary kiss to Welsh 'soil' on the airport apron, he was greeted by Archbishop of Cardiff John Murphy and many other dignitaries. His entourage included Cardinal Basil Hume, and during the welcoming ceremonies the Pope apparently said to Eddie Maloney, 'Thank you Mr Maloney for allowing me to use your airport.' An impromptu walkabout at the airport set the atmosphere for the day, but delayed the start of a mass in front of 150,000 people at Pontcanna Fields. Part of his homily was delivered in Welsh, but also Pope John Paul's message said, 'Today the Bishop of Rome greets the people of Wales for the first time in their own beautiful land. It is a great joy for me to be with you here in Cardiff.' The Pope was then granted the Freedom of the City at a lunch in the grounds of Cardiff Castle by Lord Mayor Phil Dunleavy before moving on to Ninian Park to address a national youth rally of more than 35,000 young people from all twenty-one dioceses of England and Wales.

Famous names galore have passed through Rhoose Airport on official and unofficial visits to the principality. Henry Kissinger, US Secretary of State, arrived aboard one of the US Presidential Boeing 707s to visit Prime Minister Jim Callaghan and in 1991 New Zealand's Prime Minister Jim Bolger arrived, followed soon after by Prince Rainier of Monaco and, in 1993, the Aga Khan. In May 1998 Emperor Akihito and Empress Michiko were on a state visit to the UK – this visit embraced the Welsh capital, where they were hosted by HRH the Prince of Wales. They had been given the use of a Queen's Flight BAe146 (ZE701) whilst in the UK and this arrived at Rhoose Airport carrying the emperor and empress, plus other officials, before being driven from the airport apron in one of the Queen's Rolls-Royces, the Japanese flag fluttering from its roof, to Cardiff and a day of official engagements. Shortly after, on 16 June, one of the world's most famous statesmen used Rhoose Airport: the South African President Nelson Mandela, then eighty years old, who was in town to receive the Freedom of the City of Cardiff in a ceremony in the grounds of Cardiff Castle on the final day of the European Union summit, taking place at nearby City Hall. He was greeted at the airport by the Lord Lieutenant of Glamorgan, Peter Hain MP, and watched from above by the Goodyear airship. HRH Lady Diana, Princess of Wales, visited Rhoose on 3 June 1995 but must have

HRH Princess of Wales Lady Diana arrives aboard Queen's Flight BAe146 ZE700 in the early evening of 3 June 1995 (in stereotypical Welsh June weather!) en route to the Concert of Hope for Ty Hafan Children's Hospice. The star performer was Luciano Pavarotti, who had arrived the day before from Rimini in CL-600 VR-BQA. (Malcolm Bradbury)

wondered where she'd arrived at. Disembarking from a Queen's Flight BAe146 (ZE700) from Northolt, the weather was so awful, with wind and driving rain, even the airport's official photographer failed to take any photos of the event. She was in town to attend the Concert of Hope in Cardiff in aid of Ty Hafan Children's Hospice, of which Lady Diana was a patron – she departed later that evening to Heathrow. Joining her at the concert was Luciano Pavarotti, who arrived at Rhoose the day before in a CL-600 Challenger executive jet (VR-BQA) from Rimini in Italy. Tony Blair breezed in to Rhoose aboard an RAF Northolt-based BAe125-700 (ZD621) on 26 October 1999 for a meeting with Welsh Assembly ministers. He was met at the airport by Jane Hutt, who had just been elected to the Welsh Assembly, now Assembly Minister for the Vale of Glamorgan, and TBI's managing director for the airport at the time, Albert Harrison.

The aprons of Rhoose Airport have not only been trodden by famous people, but by many famous and unusual aircraft. Concorde's visits rank highly in the diversity stakes, and its charters are dealt with here rather than Chapter 6. Sunday 21 October 1979 saw tens of thousands of people engulf Rhoose Airport for a sight of the first Concorde to land. The aircraft was F-BVFD, an Air France aircraft which had been chartered by Cwmbran Travel for a 'trip around the bay' – the Bay of Biscay. Concorde visits to Rhoose became fairly frequent, all on charters of varying durations. One was in August 1993 when a British Airways example touched down, G-BOAC. However, when Concorde was eventually retired from service in 2003, Rhoose was one of the UK's airports on the farewell tour itinerary on 23 October 2003. Having visited Belfast and Manchester on previous days, it was a cold, clear and blustery day as Capt. Chris Norris, First Officer Peter Benn and Flight Engineer Dick Maher, landed G-BOAC on Rhoose's runway 12. After landing and with the Welsh flag now fluttering from the captain's side window, 'AC taxied to a spot on the south-east apron for its farewell to Wales. The Concorde took off later to return to Heathrow before its farewell to Scotland at Edinburgh the next day. Air France had retired their Concordes earlier in 2003, and BA's last commercial Concorde service was flown the following day.

An equally revolutionary aircraft to Concorde, but from a different era, stopped off at Rhoose in June 1982 on the last leg of its ferry flight from the USA to the UK (Fairoaks). This was the

Boeing 247 (N18E), the first of the modern airliners, capable of carrying ten passengers and a low-wing, all-metal monoplane, the spur to the development of the Douglas DC-1, DC-2 and DC-3. The aircraft was en route to the Science Museum collection and can still be seen preserved (non-airworthy) at Wroughton, near Swindon. In the same genre the 26 September 1994 arrival of Lufthansa's superbly restored Junker Ju 52 tri-motor airliner D-AQUI of the 1930s era was equally significant, originally delivered to the airline on 10 April 1936 as a float-plane; the aircraft flew again after restoration in April 1986 for Lufthansa public relations work, and is still flying in 2011. It stopped at Rhoose in transit from Dublin to Bristol and flew a late-morning, thirty-minute pleasure flight before its leisurely hop across the Bristol Channel to Bristol. On 30 June 1978 the huge, droning, slow-flying Goodyear Airship (N2A), or 'blimp' as the Americans call them, arrived to provide aerial newsreel coverage of an event in central Cardiff. It was a real air traffic conundrum, but twenty years later it was back, coincident with Nelson Mandela's visit. The stability of these aircraft make them excellent aerial camera plat-forms, as well as a great advertising billboard. Less obvious as a hugely significant visitor was the Federal Aviation Administration (FAA) Boeing 727 (N40) that was based at Rhoose for a week during August 1995, fitted with sophisticated GPS equipment and in joint RVSM (reduced vertical separation monitoring) trials with the UK's Civil Aviation Authority (CAA), aimed at establishing reduced-height separation of airliners on the transatlantic airways – this aircraft had visited prior to this as well, and in September 1993 was assisted in its research and evaluation work by RAF Boscombe Down's BAC1-11 XX105. Equipment on board the 727 was used in conjunction with a ground-mounted Height-Monitoring Unit (HMU) radar located at Strumble in west Wales, one of only three or four in the whole of Western Europe. The result of these trials, implemented in 1997, was that far more airspace became available for transatlantic airline operations with a 1,000ft vertical separation established and they also helped to make the operations of many airlines more cost effective.

Going back several decades in Rhoose's history, and when small or light aircraft were a common feature at the airport, was the airport's strategic location in the western approaches of the UK, a stepping stone for aircraft transiting to and from the Republic of Ireland and requiring a stopover for fuel and customs clearance – this was prior to the days of the several Prevention of Terrorism Acts and necessity for police special branch clearance for aircraft from Ireland entering the UK. Over the years, hundreds of light aircraft of many nationalities used Rhoose for this purpose. The filming of the epic movie *The Blue Max*, a First World War adven-ture movie, saw some flimsy 'wood and wire' aircraft stopping off on 27 November 1965 on their way back to France – Stampe biplane F-BBIT and Morane Saulnier MS.317 F-BGMR

A youthful Tony Blair arrives at Rhoose in the late 1990s in an RAF BAe125-700, met by Jane Hutt (now an Assembly Minister) and Airport Managing Director Albert Harrison. (Cardiff Airport)

Thousands of spectators turned out to witness the historic first visit by a Concorde, Air France's F-BVFD, in October 1979. (Geoff Jones)

The sleek lines of Concorde G-BOAC, at Rhoose in August 1993, will surely never be matched in any commercial airliner. (Geoff Jones)

Iconic and unusual Boeing 247 N18E which transited in June 1982 on delivery from the USA to Fairoaks and the Science Museum Collection at Wroughton, where it is still on display. (Geoff Jones)

The airport board with Managing Director Eddie Maloney are dwarfed by the Goodyear Airship N2A moored in the late 1970s. At the far left is Cllr Ted Davies (Vice Chairman of the Airport Joint Committee), then to the right of him is Bob Skinner (airport Publicity/Marketing Officer). Next is probably Lord Haycock and to the right, in front of Eddie Maloney, is Cllr Hayden Tabram (Chairman of the Airport Joint Committee). (Eddie Maloney Collection)

were clearing customs and fuelling on their way to Dijon. Shot on location at Baldonnell in southern Ireland, the film necessitated the construction of several First World War replica aircraft at various workshops in the UK and France and then the ferry of these aircraft to Ireland. Another classic arrival was on 13 July 1967, when the Swiss-registered NA Ryan Navion 4 HB-ESF stopped briefly for fuel and customs en route from Basle to Dublin.

Rhoose's strategic location in the western approaches to the UK provided many ferry pilots with a stopping-off or arrival point whilst on long-distance ferry flights. In the 1970s, as Britten Norman were churning out BN-2 Islanders from their Isle of Wight factory, some of these dropped in to Rhoose prior to their ferry flights west across the Atlantic for Jonas Aircraft, the US distributor. In the opposite direction, in 1970 three Short Skyvans on a delivery flight from their factory in Belfast to the Indonesian Air Force called in for fuel on 4 August, their next stop after Rhoose being Bordeaux in western France. On 27 February 1979 a North American TB-25N 'Mitchell' (N9455Z), former Second World War bomber, stopped off overnight en route from Blackbushe in Hampshire to Dublin – then on 1 March a second TB-25 (N9115Z) stopped briefly at Rhoose before continuing to Dublin, film work in Ireland the reason for the exodus. Soon after on 2 February 1981, although not landing but doing a low flyby, was the former Antilles Air Boats Short Sandringham flying boat VP-LVE (ex-N158C,VH-BRC)). Under threat of scrapping after the death of its owner, former Antilles chief pilot Ron Gillies acquired the aircraft, raised money and ferried it from Puerto Rico to Ireland in October 1980. When it flew by at Rhoose it was on its very last flight, to Calshot, where it was beached. It is now preserved in the Southampton Hall of Aviation.

The military have also been regulars at Rhoose. From *Armée de l'Air* (French air force) MS Paris jets during early French rugby airlifts, to RAF Jet Provosts and Hunters at 1960's Welsh Air Rally and, much more recently, on 3 August 1993, a pair of Mirage 2000 fighters after a display at St Mawgan and choosing Rhoose as they didn't want to land on St Mawgan's shortened

This Federal Aviation
Administration (FAA)
Boeing 727 was used
in August 1995 in
conjunction with the
UK's CAA to evaluate
reduced vertical separation
in the airways and airspace
over the North Atlantic.
(Geoff Jones)

Avril Brown (left) and Bethan
Summers, who worked in the
general office at the airport,
pose next to *Armée de l'Air*
Mirage 2000, one of two that
diverted en route from St
Mawgan Air Day in Cornwall
to their base at St Saveur/
Luxeuil on 3 August 1993.
(Malcolm Bradbury)

Spanish government
officials used this Fuerza
Aerea Española Boeing
707 (4510 T17-1) to fly in
for the European Leaders'
Summit in Cardiff in June
1998. (Malcolm Bradbury)

A European foreign ministers' conference at Celtic Manor resort in September 2005 brought a varied array of official aircraft, including the Republic Hrvatska (Croatia) CL-600 9A-CRO and Hellenic Republic (Greece) Embraer ERJ-135. (Geoff Jones)

runway to avoid deploying their landing chutes and then having to re-pack them. Not long after this, on 1 September, a huge USAF Boeing B-52H (61-0020 call-sign SLAM13) did an overshoot at Rhoose en route from St Mawgan to Fairford. When St Athan was closed the 60 Squadron Buccaneer S.2 XT276 arrived on 4 August 1980 from RAF Laarbruch in Germany to be road-run to Saints. Percival Pembroke also arrived from RAF Wildenrath to act as crew ferry for the Buccaneer. Another Buccaneer XV161 operated in the opposite direction that December, flying back from Rhoose to RAF Honington. The last in service, airworthy RAF Avro Vulcan (XH558) did a run-through at Rhoose on 23 March 1993, and many RAF Hawks have dropped in or flown by, with many RAF C-130 Hercules aircraft using the airport's Instrument Landing System (ILS) during training approaches. On 3 July 1994 XV209 undertook aerial sorties with local school children.

Luftwaffe aircraft including Noratlas, C-160D Transall freighters, a former East German Tupolev Tu-154, Boeing 707 and Airbus A310 aircraft, were also frequent visitors Rhoose over a span of thirty-five years, related to the panzer tank training agreement and training which took place on the Castlemartin artillery ranges in Pembrokeshire. The first recorded Luftwaffe flights to Rhoose were in the summer of 1963, when several Nord Noratlas aircraft diverted from their intended destination at RNAS Brawdy near St David's in west Wales. When Brawdy closed for operational flying in 1991, Rhoose took over as the air head for many of the flights up until the cessation of the training work at Castlemartin in October 1996 – the flights would be approximately every ten days during the 'live' tank season between June and December. The very last support flights were on 15 October 1996 and included the unique and unusual VFW-614 twin-jet passenger aircraft, plus a CH-53G 'Jolly Green Giant' transport helicopter which carried senior German army officers to attend the closing ceremony at Pembroke.

The President of Spain's Boeing 707 (Fuerza Aerea Española) arrived at Rhoose on 15 June 1998 during a European leaders' summit, plus many other quasi-military presidential aircraft: in

'Rook', a USAF stealth U-2 (80-1069) slides south-east along the line of runway 12 on 29 January 1993 after a fly-by at St Athan. (Malcolm Bradbury)

September 2005 a European foreign ministers summit, hosted by the UK's Foreign Secretary Jack Straw, was held at Celtic Manor, Newport, attracting an eclectic mix of official aircraft. These included a ROMBAC BAC1-11 with the Romanian minister; a CL-600 with the Slovenian minister; a Falcon 2000 with the Republic of Bulgaria's minister; and a Yak-40 with the Polish minister. On 17 June 1999 a USAF Rockwell B-1B long-range strategic bomber (85-0091/EL) from the 2nd AEG/100th AEW temporarily based at RAF Fairford and operating missions in the war in the Balkans, did an approach and run-through at Rhoose. It was on a local training flight from Fairford, slotted in between operational sorties over Kosovo. Picking the crème de la crème, though, is a subjective choice, but maybe the flyby of a USAF U-2 stealth reconnaissance aircraft (80-1069) using the call-sign 'Rook' on 29 January 1993 could be it, when, on a pre-planned overshoot of runway 26 at St Athan, it was requested by air traffic control at Rhoose to do a flyby along runway 12. The crew obliged! Or was it the 28 April 1994 over-flight at approximately 3,000ft of a Russian Antonov An-30 'Clank' photographic/survey twin turboprop? It didn't land at Rhoose but, using the call-sign 'Osprey 99', was exercising the privileges of the Open Skies Treaty signed between NATO and the Warsaw Pact countries, which permitted the aircraft of each signature state to fly over the territory of any other signatory state.

In September 2007, with RAF St Athan closed for the weekend, Rhoose was able to welcome a quartet of RAF aircraft that were displaying over Swansea seafront. Specialist ground equipment was shipped in for the two BAe Systems Typhoon or Eurofighters of 29(R) OCU Squadron, who made several visits and one sortie to a display at Southend. The two Hawk trainers were from 4 FTS at RAF Valley in special RAF promotional colours for the ninetieth anniversary of the RAF and also part of the Swansea display. However, all these were eclipsed on 16 September by a flypast in V formation from west to east along the line of runway 12 of the RAF Red Arrows. The 'Reds' have been not infrequent visitors to Rhoose: a run-through and break en route to Exeter on 26 August 1994 celebrated the first time Rhoose had handled 1 million passengers in a twelve-month period – airport managing director at the time Graham Greaves undoubtedly had some part to play in this event. Another 'Reds' visit occurred on a May evening in 1997 when they were displaying at a seafront air show at Kidwelly. Rhoose's proximity to RAF St Athan has many military implications. With the 2007 closure of the DARA (Defence Aviation Repair Agency) fast jet maintenance facility at St Athan, RAF aircraft that would have diverted to Saints regularly select Rhoose as their diversion.

12

WHAT'S IN A NAME, CURRENT AIRPORT FACILITIES, THE FUTURE

As recently as 2008, Abertis TBI, the owners of the airport at Rhoose, sought to bring the name of the airport up to date. The vogue for renaming airports started in the US, with names such as John Wayne for Orange County Airport in southern California, John F. Kennedy for one of New York's airports and William B. Hartsfield for Atlanta's international airport, named after a city mayor. The trend moved to the UK and Liverpool became John Lennon and Belfast City George Best – what to call Cardiff's airport? Well, the headline writers had a field day, and the consultants employed by TBI inevitably milked it – Welsh stars and celebrities were top of the list, Tom Jones International, Richard Burton International, Shirley Bassey International and even Gavin and Stacey International were all suggested, some more seriously than others. More gravitas was urged by some, with homage to Welsh forefathers such as Prince Owain Glyndwr or NHS founder Aneurin Bevan. The upshot, decided in 2009, was plain and simply 'Cardiff Airport – Maes Awyr Caerdydd', with even the vogue word 'international' excluded, but also a new visually different logo.

It started life as RAF Rhoose as part of 53 Operational Training Unit, with none of the glamour or legend that is attached to some more iconic and legendary RAF stations. Rhoose has passed through the ownership of many organisations, from the state, to local authority, to private, and each new owner has sought to stamp their signature on their piece of aviation real estate.

The history of names used for the airport is as follows:

1942–52	RAF Rhoose
1952–65	Cardiff (Rhoose) Airport
1965–74	Glamorgan (Rhoose) Airport
1974–95	Cardiff-Wales Airport
1995–2009	Cardiff International Airport
2009–Present	Cardiff Airport – Maes Awyr Caerdydd

British Airways Maintenance Cardiff (BAMC), a wholly owned subsidiary of BA, is located on the north side of the airport and is noted as 'the most prominent structure in the whole of South Wales'. Rhoose was chosen by British Airways for this prestigious facility from a shortlist that included Singapore, Liverpool, Glasgow and Bristol. Rhoose was chosen because there was a large greenfield site on the edge of an established airport with a suitable runway for 'wide-bodies', plus availability of a pool of skilled local labour.

British Airways Maintenance Cardiff, despite the frequent disparaging remarks about the prominence and the 'out-of-context' huge hangar, continues a long tradition of airliner

The approach road to the airport in 2009, showing the airport's new name: Cardiff Airport – Maes Awyr Caerdydd. (Geoff Jones)

maintenance at Rhoose. This started with Cambrian Airways, becoming British Airways after their takeover of Cambrian, and more briefly BAF (British Air Ferries) Maintenance. British Air Ferries maintenance's most unusual contract was in August 1982 when they carried out work on the DC-8 5A-DJD of Tripoli, Libya-based United African Airlines, a big departure from their bread-and-butter Viscount work.

It was in June 1990 that the proposal to build a huge, new £70 million hangar for BA to maintain its Boeing 747 fleet was first aired in public. By February 1993 BA's Project DragonFly opened for business, but was not formally opened until June by HRH the Prince of Wales; the revival of BA's presence at Rhoose continued. The BA site occupies 70 acres and the floor area of the main hangar is 22,000m², the support and administration buildings at its rear a further 16,000m², and it was intended to employ over 1,000 people, although now nearer 650. The huge building has a three-bay Boeing 747 capacity with two additional 'nose-in' facilities for interior modifications, and shielded engine run-up pans to its south-west. The facility has been used primarily for BA's in-house maintenance needs, but over the years some third-party maintenance has been carried out, for Air New Zealand, Corsair, Kalitta, Alitalia and Canadian. The Air New Zealand Boeing 747-400 (ZK-NZT) arrived at Rhoose direct from Auckland, New Zealand on 22 August 1996, probably the longest flight inbound to Rhoose ever – after work by BAMC it departed back to Auckland on 25 September. In December 2002 two ex-BA Boeing 777-200s were resident and painted in the colours of Khalifa; Air Algerie received pre-lease maintenance prior to the start of a five-year lease with that airline. The prestige that the BAMC facility affords to Rhoose and to Wales helped secure Cardiff as the September 2003 venue for MRO Europe, the world's premier event for aircraft maintenance, repair and overhaul organisations. Over 2,000 delegates from around the world attended the conference and exhibition at the CIA between 16 and 18 September, many of them travelling to the event via Rhoose.

British Airways' Boeing 747s of all series have been regular visitors to BAMC for 'heavy maintenance' and internal fitting/refurbishment. From February 2008 BA's Boeing 767-300 series aircraft have also been handled here – by 2010 some of the airline's ageing 747-400s were placed into storage at the airport and, before this in 2002, B747-100 G-BDXC was the first to be parted out and scrapped at Rhoose. BA Boeing 777s also use the BAMC facility: on 10 July 2010 Rhoose welcomed the very first BA Boeing 777-336ER to touch down in the UK, G-STBA flying in direct from Boeing at Seattle's Everett/Paine Field, for its premium, business and first-class cabins to be fitted out. It also conducted extensive trials from Rhoose of new on-board navigation equipment, prior to flying onwards to Heathrow on 18 August and its entry to service on 31 August on a BA Heathrow to Mumbai schedule. The second BA B777-336ER ('BB) arrived at Rhoose on 31 August and left for Heathrow on 20 September.

Wales Air Museum

This was founded at Rhoose in 1975 from the embryo of the South Wales Historical Aircraft Preservation Society (SWHAPS), which had been founded in 1967 by Mal Sketchley. Some aircraft were already on site at Rhoose before 1975, the DH Vampire T.11 WZ425 arriving in May 1973. The Wales Air Museum's objective was to give Wales its only aircraft museum which would be open to the general public throughout the year. Close links were maintained with RAF St Athan, where an extremely active aircraft preservation unit operated.

Wales Air Museum's first site, made available by the airport authority, was on the west side of the northern access road close to the current catering and police buildings. The museum's master plan was to first establish an outdoor display of a small number of aircraft, then to move to a larger display area with picnic site and aircraft viewing area and finally to erect a building to house soft-skinned aircraft, engines and related memorabilia. During the late 1970s the museum moved quickly through the initial stages, acquiring up to two dozen aircraft in the process. Most of these were donated to WAM, but three aircraft were loaned by the USAF and a Hunter by British Aerospace. Appropriately, a Vickers V808 Viscount (G-AOJC) in later Cambrian colours was donated after it retired from service in 1975. The fuselage of another Viscount, G-ANRS – which had been located on the southern side of the airport as a cabin trainer marked G-WHIZ – was also moved to the site, appearing in Cambrian colours and at one time in Dan-Air colours, marked fictitiously as 'G-ARBY'. A Vickers Varsity T-Mk 1 (WJ944), which last served with No.6 FTS at RAF Finningley, was flown to Rhoose on 13 April 1976 and then parked at the museum. Most of the other exhibits were former military aircraft, the exceptions being the remains of the Percival Proctor V G-AHTE and the extremely rare forward fuselage of Avro Ashton high-altitude research jet WE670, a type developed from the Avro Tudor that had been registered G-AJKA. These remains were with British Aerospace at Dunsfold, used for training police dogs, but were moved by road to Rhoose in June 1980. With the retirement of Avro Vulcans from service, WAM acquired XM569 – this was flown to Rhoose from RAF Waddington on 2 February 1983 by Squadron Leader Neil McDougal. In hindsight, an incredible and varied selection of aircraft were assembled by WAM at Rhoose (see below) – the sheer magnitude and variety probably helped contribute to their demise.

Cambrian Viscount G-AMNZ was leased to Air France from 1966–69 along with G-AMOC to fly the airline's London Heathrow to Lille schedule – it is seen here in the maintenance hangar at Rhoose, with Cyril Tomlinson just visible cowering inside the rear door. (Morley Williams)

When the land used by WAM was required by the airport, the museum had to move lock, stock and barrel across the road to an area now used for one of the long-stay car parks. Not all the exhibits could be moved and this was probably the thin end of the wedge which saw the end of the museum in the 1990s. Some aircraft were scrapped on site in 1991, but most of the exhibits were scrapped on site between 1996 and 1998, or disposed of to other museums around the country.

WAM Exhibits at Rhoose (with thanks to SWAG)

Auster AOP.9	WZ662	Army Air Corps (became G-BKVK)
Avro Ashton 2	WB491	To Newark Air Museum
Avro Vulcan B.1	XA903	Rolls-Royce (nose only)
Avro Vulcan B.2	XM569	RAF
BAC Jet Provost T.3	XN458	RAF (also painted as XN594)
BAC Lightning F.53	ZF578	Royal Saudi AF
Blackburn Buccaneer S.1	XN928	Royal Navy
Dassault Mystere IV	59	French Air Force
De Havilland Venom FB.4	WR539	RAF
De Havilland Sea Venom FAW.21	WW217	Royal Navy
De Havilland Sea Venom FAW.22	XG737	Royal Navy
De Havilland Venom NF.3	WX788	ex-DH at Hawarden
De Havilland Vampire T.11	WZ425	RAF
De Havilland Sea Vixen FAW.2	XN650	Royal Navy
English Electric Canberra B.2	WP515	RAF
English Electric Canberra PR.7	WH798	RAF
English Electric Canberra PR.7	WT518	RAF
English Electric Canberra T.17	WJ576	RAF
English Electric Canberra T.17	WJ581	RAF
English Electric Canberra PR.9	XH177	RAF (nose only)
Fairey Gannet ECM.6	XA903	Royal Navy
Fairey Gannet T.5	XG883	Royal Navy
Fairey Gannet AEW.3	XL449	Royal Navy – flown in 25 Sep. 1978
Gloster Meteor T.7	WL332	Royal Navy
Gloster Meteor F.8	WE925	RAF
Gloster Meteor TT.20	WM292	Royal Navy
Hawker Hunter F.51	E409	Royal Danish Air Force
Hawker Sea Hawk FGA.6	WV795	Royal Navy
Hawker Sea Hawk FGA.4	unidentified	Royal Navy
Hawker Sea Hawk FGA.6	WV826	Royal Navy (re-painted WV906)
Lockheed T-33A-1-LO	52-9963	USAF
McDonnell Douglas Phantom FGR.2	XT911	RAF (nose only)
North American F-100D Super Sabre	54-2160	USAF
Percival Proctor IV	G-AHTE	Sold in Suffolk in 1994
Percival Provost T.1	WW388	RAF (exchanged for Proctor 'TE)
Percival Pembroke C.1	WV753	RAF (burnt remains still exist)
Saunders-Roe Skeeter AOP.12	XN351	Army AC (loan – became G-BKSC)

One of the first BA Boeing 747-136s to arrive for work at BAMC, G-AWNB, outside the newly opened facility in 1995. (Geoff Jones)

Air New Zealand Boeing 747-400 ZK-NBT undergoing maintenance in the huge BAMC hangar at Rhoose in September 1996. (Malcolm Bradbury)

Stripped to bare metal, ex-Cathay 747-200F N2868R is pictured here in January 2010. (Geoff Jones)

The Avro Vulcan XM569, which was flown to Rhoose after its demobilisation by the RAF, dwarfs all the other exhibits in the Wales Air Museum collection in this 1992 picture. (Geoff Jones)

Socata MS.880B Rallye Club	G-BFTZ	Late arrival in 1992
Vickers Varsity T.1	WJ944	RAF
Vickers Valiant BK.1	XD826	RAF (nose only)
Vickers V.732 Viscount	G-ANRS (G-WHIZ)	Used by Cambrian for spares
Vickers V.808 Viscount	G-AOJC	Ex-BA
Westland Dragonfly HR.3	WG718	Royal Navy
Westland Whirlwind HAS.7	XG592	Royal Navy (now at Cowbridge)
Westland Whirlwind HAR.10	XJ409	RAF
Westland Wessex HAS.1	XM300	RAE – now at Nantgarw

Wales' aircraft-manufacturing history is largely dominated by Airbus Industries/EADS and their predecessors, including Hawker Siddeley located in North Wales. Several homebuilders of small light aircraft, built under the auspices of the PFA and LAA, have kept the spirit alive in and around the Rhoose area. However, in 1982 a microlight designed by Bill Brookes and built by BAF subsidiary Dragon Light Aircraft Ltd was built in the old Cambrian hangar – the prototype G-MMAA first flying at Rhoose on 8 July 1982 in time for its official launch at that year's Farnborough Air Show, where it was expected to sell for £4,000. Problems with the new two-cylinder 525cc Hunting engine did not help the success of the project and it is thought only six examples were built or part built.

A major departure from small-time aircraft manufacture briefly blossomed at Rhoose in the mid-1980s, with the Norman Aeroplane Company. With Welsh Development Agency (WDA) funding a large new hangar/production facility was built on the south side to manufacture the Fieldmaster agricultural aircraft; the building is still extant today, adjoining the car park used by Aeros and the Rhoose Flying Club restaurant.

The Norman Aeroplane Company (NAC) was the brainchild of Desmond Norman, half of the famous post-war duo of John Britten and Desmond Norman, whose abiding epitaph will be their twin-engine, high-wing, ten-seat utility aircraft the BN-2 Islander. When located at the Sandown on the Isle of Wight, Britten Norman designed and built the BN-3 Nymph in the 1960s, a Cessna 172-like aircraft with folding wings that didn't go in to production with Britten Norman. NDN Aircraft Ltd took over the rights to the Nymph, redesignating it the NAC1 Freelance. NDN Aircraft Ltd also designed and built the NDN.1 Firecracker, tandem, two-seat military turboprop trainer, unsuccessfully entered for the RAF's trainer competition in conjunction with Hunting Aircraft, and which was eventually won by the Shorts

Ceremony outside the Norman Aeroplane Co. (NAC) on 28 April 1987 when the CAA presented Desmond Norman with the Type Certificate for the Fieldmaster. (Geoff Jones Collection)

When this photo was taken in 1986, NAC were ramping up production of the Fieldmaster at Rhoose. (Geoff Jones)

Tucano. Another project was the NDN.6 Fieldmaster, originally designed under sponsorship that Desmond Norman had negotiated with the National Research and Development Council (NDRC). The prototype was first flown in the Isle of Wight on 17 December 1981, intended for liquid aerial crop treatment and for fire fighting with chemical retardants. NDN Aircraft Ltd opened for business at Rhoose in July 1985, full certification and production of the Fieldmaster the goal.

On 28 April 1987 Jerry Wraith, the CAA's design surveyor, came to Rhoose to present Desmond Norman with the type certificate for the Fieldmaster. Norman Aeroplane Co.'s factory was a hive of activity with just under 100 employees embarking on construction of five production versions of the Fieldmaster, plus other ancillary work on the Firecracker and Freelance aircraft. Unfortunately, NAC went into receivership in August 1988. A company called Croplease acquired the design rights to the Fieldmaster, renaming it the Firemaster 65, with work commencing at Old Sarum airfield, Wiltshire, but none of the plans came to fruition. The Rhoose factory was vacated, was let between 2005 and 2008 to Air Wales and is now used for general storage and as a hangar for a few light aircraft. A number of proposals are being considered for its future use.

The Future

All air transport is cyclical: airlines, airports and aerospace manufacturers. They mirror the economy more than anything else. The 14 per cent year-on-year decline in passenger numbers from 2009 to 2010 at Rhoose has to be viewed against overall UK figures of a 12 per cent drop in passengers, or 7.2 million fewer passengers flying. At Rhoose the reduction was due to several specific factors, including the reduction in capacity by bmibaby (approx. 200,000 passengers), the effects of the April 2010 volcanic ash cloud, market conditions and some atrocious adverse weather in the latter quarter of the year. The decline was further compounded with the 13 April 2011 announcement of bmibaby's planned withdrawal at the end of their summer 2011 services. This recent decline in passenger numbers is almost certainly just a blip and, as happened when Air Wales failed, new and established operators will certainly take over bmibaby's services.

In July 2002 the Department of Transport in association with the Welsh Assembly government published *The Future Development of Air Transport in the United Kingdom: Wales*. This was a consultation document on the future of aviation in Wales, which inevitably majored on Rhoose Airport or Cardiff International Airport as it then was. It notes that in the 2000 UK rankings, Rhoose was seventh for charter traffic from regional airports and twelfth for scheduled traffic, and confirms that Rhoose offers a range of domestic and international services, with its charter programme particularly strong for an airport of its size. Average annual growth between 1991 and 2000 was 12.7 per cent. The document forecasts that between 4 and 5.5 million passengers per annum would be likely to use Rhoose in 2030, or around three times as many passengers as in 2001. It also identifies that the main factor affecting traffic levels at Rhoose and the level of impact it has is the extent to which capacity is available at other airports in south-east England. The document showed a 'Cardiff Airport Future Master Plan' with a new terminal and a vastly increased number of aircraft parking stands, but with the existing runway 12/30 remaining as is. Four scenarios 'were introduced, the UK-Wide Constrained Scenario, the Facilitating Growth Scenario, the Fly Local Scenario and the Concentrated Growth Scenario. The last one points out that if Bristol was targeted for growth, the forecast for Rhoose would be lower … with increased leakage from the local catchment area'. In the airport *Master Plan 2006* Jon Horne, the airport MD, described the UK government's 2003 white paper, 'The Future of Air Transport', which says that '… we want to produce a world-class facility for Wales and the West'.

Unfortunately for Rhoose, the 'leakage' to Bristol and elsewhere outside the principality has indeed happened during the first decade of the twenty-first century, and the combined effects of this and a change in holiday patterns from package holidays to self-booked holidays, rises in fuel prices and therefore fares, and specifically in 2010 the effects on air travel of the Icelandic volcanic ash cloud, all impacted on Rhoose's traffic. However, some regional airports have reported growth over the same period, so Rhoose's traffic must embrace factors in addition to those above.

A perennial point of discussion for decades has been surface access links to Rhoose Airport. The 2002 publication identified that if traffic was to grow as then predicted then there would be a number of associated surface access issues. The Welsh Assembly government commissioned a study to assess road traffic demand and network capacity at Culverhouse Cross, Cardiff, the A4232 trunk road and access roads to the airport – 'trunking' of this road and relief of congestion at Culverhouse Cross was proposed. A dedicated rail link to the airport was also considered unlikely, but advocated the reopening of the Vale of Glamorgan railway line to passenger trains, with a bus link from Rhoose station to the airport. This happened.

However, many consider a new road necessary to link the airport with the M4 to help promote airport accessibility and growth. In a 2006 feasibility study, the '5-Mile Lane Option to M4 junction 34', was favoured. In 2008 a Trunk Road Forward Programme stated, referring to this 5-Mile Lane option, that '… this work should be high ranking and programmed ready to start between April 2011 and April 2014'. The SEWTA (South East Wales Transport Alliance) draft Regional Transport Plan submitted to the Welsh Assembly in December 2008 calls for 'improved sustainable access to Cardiff Airport'.

A new access road will not be Rhoose's panacea. The airport owners are working diligently to raise the profile of the airport, to promote new business, attract new airlines and routes and increase passenger numbers. Regardless of the success, Cardiff's airport at Rhoose will continue towards its centenary year in 2042 and embrace changes in air transport technology to the benefit of Wales, Cardiff and the Welsh population. And hopefully along the way the Welsh Assembly, the airport owners, its passengers and the thousands of people whose livelihoods depends on the airport will not forget the rich history of this significant piece of Welsh aeronautical real estate as described in this book, all of which has helped to make Cardiff Airport at Rhoose what it is today.

APPENDIX 1

AIRLINES THAT HAVE OPERATED TO RHOOSE

Scheduled

Air Anglia (following their takeover of Air Wales)	1979
Aer Arann	2006–current
Air Ecosse (flew some Dan-Air City Link services)	1983
Air Florida (DC-10 flights to Miami via Prestwick)	1981–82
Aer Lingus	1952–77
Air France-Brit Air (CDG route taken over by Manx)	1990–92
Air Kilroe	1993–96
Air Southwest	2006–07
(recommended Newquay-Newcastle via Rhoose Jan 2011)	2011
Air UK (also Herald schedules in 1979)	1988–90
Air Wales (1)	1977–79
Air Wales (2)	2000–06
American Trans Air (ATA) (flights to New York JFK)	1989–90
	9 July to 10 September 1996
BAC Express (overnight freight)	1995–2000
Blue Islands Airline	2007
bmibaby	2002–11
Britannia Airways (seat only availability on charter flights)	1982–2000
British Air Ferries (BAF) – regular Herald flight to/from Ostend	1978
	1979–86
British Air Services (see Cambrian)	1967–74
British Airways (see Cambrian/BAS and British Regional and Manx)	
British Midland Airways (BMA) – formerly Derby Airways	1960–69
	1972–73
British Regional (Manx)	2002–04
British Westpoint Airways	1964–66
Brown Air Services (Gulfstream 1 to Leeds/Newcastle) (see Capital)	1986–87
Brymon Airways – to Plymouth	1974–75
	1988–92
Cambrian Airways (originally Cambrian Air Services)	1954–75
Capital Airlines (originally Brown Air)	1987–90
Celtic Airways (cargo/mail operator) (took over from Gill Air)	1991–93
Centreline Air Services (operating Dan-Air service to Glasgow)	1982

Channel Express (Cargo/mail operator) (not continuous operations)	1982–2000
CP Air (Canadian Pacific)	1977–83
Dan-Air (see Metropolitan) (when schedules ceased in 1986, charters until 1992)	1960–92
Eastern Airways	2006–current
Euroair (including Cardiff–Chester schedule)	1981–88
flybe	2007–current
Highland Airways (Welsh Office PSO service to Anglesey)	2007–2010
(Highland ceased trading on 24 March 2010 – PSO service suspended pending new operator)	
Inter European Airways (taken over by Airtours)	1987–93
Jersey Airlines (service ceased on 21 March)	1958–59
Jersey European Airways (JEA) – Jersey-Rhoose–Ostend service	1977, 1979/80, 1984/85
(ceased schedules 8 November 1985, continued mail flights until Jan 1986, resumed 1990, then 1999–2000)	
Kestrel International – Viscount service for Dan-Air via Bristol to IofM	1972
KLM Cityhopper (initially flown on inter-line basis with Dan-Air)	1979–current
Knight Air (EMB-110 operator to Leeds/Newcastle)	1994
Lease Air (cargo service with DC-3s)	1979 and 1982
Leisure International Airways (Air UK subsidiary with B767s)	mid-1990s
Loganair (Twin Otter schedules to Glasgow)	1966–67
Manx Airlines (BA franchisee from 1995)	1991–2002
Manx2.com	2010–current
Mayflower Air Services (ex-Scillonian Air Services) – Aero Commander 500A	1964
Metropolitan Airways (subsidiary of Alderney Air Ferries – franchise of Dan-Air)	1982–85
McAlpine Aviation (Jetstream service to Brussels)	1985
Monarch (also regular BAC1-11 flights 1972/73/74/75 and 1977)	1989–94
Netherlines (Amsterdam schedule taken over by KLM Cityhopper)	1986–89
Reed Aviation (cargo/night mail flights)	1997–98
Ryanair	1987–2006
Severn Airways (Newquay service with Dove and Aztec)	1975
Swansea Airways (Swansea–Shannon via Rhoose for customs with a Percival Prentice G-APJE and Rapide G-AGJG)	1960–61
Zoom Airlines (Canada) – first flight on 2 May 2005	2005–08

Charter (only regular operations listed – many one-off or intermittent charter operators not included here; many charters are also seasonal)

Adria (Yugoslavian) Airways	1988–90
Aegean Airlines	2005
Aeroflot	1984–87
Aer Turas (Cambrian chartered one of their DC-4s)	1966
Air Anglia (series of oil-related F.27 services)	1972–73
Air Atlanta Icelandic	1995
Air Atlantis	1989
Air Columbus (took over from TAP to Faro, Portugal)	1986, 1987/88, 1990, 1992/93
Air Ecosse	1980
Air Europe	1979–91
Air Europa (Spain)	1987–2000
Air Foyle (cargo only)	1995
Air Malta	1981–98
Air Transat	1995–97
Air Yugoslavia	1990
Air 2000	1989, 1995–96, 2000
Airtours International Airways (acquired by MyTravel)	1990–2002
Airways International Cymru (airline of Tony Clemo's Red Dragon Travel)	1984–88

Spanish charter airline Hispania's inaugural Caravelle service from Rhoose in June 1983. (Geoff Jones)

For one season only in 1997 Nouvelair Tunisie operated charters to Monastir with their leased MD-83s, EI-CNO (pictured) and EI-CBO. (Geoff Jones Collection)

Spanish charter airline Spantax, renowned for its fleet of fuel-thirsty Convair CV-990 jets, used Douglas DC-9-14s (EC-CGZ pictured in 1981), but also DC-8-63s for IT charter services to the Balearic Islands. (Geoff Jones)

One of Court Line's brightly coloured BAC1-11s G-AXMI in summer 1971. (John Mead)

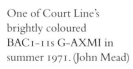

Airworld (charter airline for Thomas Cook travel group)	1994–98
Ambassador Airways	1994
Astraeus Airlines	2006
Autair (series of Saturday Herald charters to Ostend)	1967
Aviaco	1977–84
Aviogenex	1979–91
Aurigny Air Services (miscellaneous charters, but not continuous ops)	1985–95
Balkan Bulgarian Airlines and BH Air (Balkan Holidays)	1979–2007
BCAL (British Caledonian) (series of BAC1-11 charters)	1971–73
BEA (British European Airways) (weekly BAC1-11 and Trident charters to Palma)	1973
Britannia Airways (now operating through mergers, etc., as Thomsonfly)	1970–current
British Island Airways (BIA)	1989
British Mediterranean ('ghost flights' to and from Heathrow to retain the airline's slots)	
British Midland Airways	1994, 1998–2000
British World	1998–99
Busy Bee (weekly charters to and from Norway)	September 1982, 1983
Caledonian Airways (BCAL also operated BAC1-11s 1971–73)	1993
Canafrican (MD-83 operator)	1987
Channel Airways (springtime Viscount charters to Rotterdam/Amsterdam)	1967
Court Line (IT charters with brightly coloured BAC1-11s)	1970–74
Cronus (Greek operator)	2000
Cyprus Airways	1989
Delta Air Transport (Belgian charter airline)	1980–83
Dominie Airways (DH.89 subsidiary of Treffield flying ad hoc charters)	mid-1966
Euravia (became Britannia in Aug 1964 – see Thomsonfly)	1964
Eurocypria Airlines (not continuous operations during this period)	1993–2010
Excalibur Airways (Airbus A320s)	1994–96
First Choice Airways (formerly Air 2000, merged with TUI, then Thomson)	2004–07
Flightline (Southend-based BAe146 charter operator)	1997
Flying Colours	1999
Futura	1991–2000
Gill Airways (cargo operator)	1988–90
Globe Air (Swiss charter airline – ski charters to Interlaken/Sion)	winter 1966
Hispania (Caravelle and B737s)	1983–88
Iberworld	1999
Icelandair (several months of services, Iceland to Las Palmas via Rhoose)	1989
Inex Adria	1989
Intersun Havacilik – Sunways Airlines (Turkish MD-83/B757 charter airline)	1995–97
Invicta Airlines (bulb-field DC-4 charters to Rotterdam)	1967
JAT (Jugoslavenski Aerotransport)	1979–86
JMC Air (the integration of Flying Colours and Caledonian Airways)	1999–2006
Kestrel International Airways (using Viscount G-AVJB to Isle of Man)	1972
Leisure International Airways (Air UK subsidiary flying B767s)	mid-1990s
Lloyd International (series of 'bulb charters' to Holland)	1970
LTE Spain	1992, 1994
Meridian (Spanish MD-83 operator)	1991
Morton Air Services (in association with Gatwick–Swansea schedule)	1959–68
My Travel (and MyTravel Lite) (see Airtours) – acquired by Thomas Cook	
Nationair (Toronto DC-8 and B747 charters)	1987, 1990–92
NorFly (Norwegian charter airline)	1981
NortJet (B737 flights to/from Ibiza and Gerona)	1988–89
Nouvelair Tunisie (MD-83 charters to Monastir, Tunis)	1997

Oasis/Andalusair (Spanish charter operator)	1994–96
Orion Airways (Horizon Travel B737 charter airline purchased by Britannia)	1979–88
Onurair (Turkish holiday charter airline)	1999–current
Overseas National Airways (series of transatlantic charters)	1974
Paramount Airways (Bristol-based MD-83 operator)	1987–89
Pegasus	1995–96
Peters Aviation (charters to Rotterdam)	1975
Sabre Airways (UK charter operator)	1994–95
South West Aviation (ad hoc charters and regular Isle of Man flights)	1970–1972
Spanair	1988–2000
Spantax	1981–87
Sterling European	1994–95
Sunways	1995, 1997
Tarom (Romanian BAC1-11 airline)	1979–80
Thomsonfly (originated at Euravia and Britannia Airways)	2004–current
Thomas Cook Airlines (renamed JMC) (earlier operated 1995 only)	2003–current
Titan Airways	1993
Transamerica Airlines (US airline operating DC-8s)	August 1982
Transeuropa (Spanish charter operator with Caravelles)	1979–82
Trans European Airways (Swansea based using a Rapide G-ALBA, then moved to Coventry and Gatwick)	1959–60
Transwede	1995
Treffield International Airways (Viscounts for Hourmont Holidays)	1967
Tunisair	1989
Tyrolean Airways (ski charters to Innsbruck)	1998–2000
VIA (Bulgarian airline operating Tupolev Tu-154s)	1995–99
VIVA Air	1994, 1997–99
Wardair (Canada)	1984–88
Worldways	1986–90

Grateful thanks to Mike Freshney for much of the above data.

PASSENGER AND MOVEMENTS STATISTICS 1958–2010

Year	Scheduled Passengers	Charter Passengers	Total Passengers	Annual Growth	Movements Total (all)	Annual Growth	Freight (Tonnes)
1958			46,357		18,018		
1959					20,322	+13%	
1960					19,232	-5%	
1961					21,588	+12%	
1962	No data available						
1963					14,892		
1964					15,685	+5%	
1965					20,708	+32%	
1966					22,516	+9%	
1967					28,646	+27%	
1968					30,432	+6%	
1969					22,631 (no Dec. data)		
1970					26,141		
1971					27,441 (no Dec. data)		
1972–75	No data available						
1976			192,300		42,700		419
1977			208,500	+8.4%	36,500	-14.5%	334
1978			234,200	+12%	36,400	-0%	243
1979			253,500	+8%	39,100	+7.5%	280
1980			261,300	+3%	39,500	+1%	208
1981			294,000	+12.5%	32,700	-13%	472
1982			360,300	+22.5%	35,700	+9%	559
1983			383,300	+6%	38,500	+8%	152
1984			428,800	+19%	43,700	+13.5%	45
1985			386,700	-10%	41,100	-6%	8
1986			**524,130**	+35.5%	40,300	-2%	156
1987			651,900	+24%	46,200	+14.5%	870
1988	No data available						
1989	94,693	603,744	732,900		60,314		2,126
1990	87,364	507,580	625,394	-15%	64,022	+6%	3,314
1991	107,496	410,698	547,192	-13%	53,109	-17%	1,734

Year	Scheduled Passengers	Charter Passengers	Total Passengers	Annual Growth	Movements Total (all)	Annual Growth	Freight (Tonnes)
1992	128,633	526,583	700,943	+28%	52,735	-1%	1,489
1993	143,173	629,516	806,225	+15%	54,346	+3%	1,654
1994	171,304	826,461	**1,033,364**	+28%	55,352	+2%	2,181
1995	183,426	855,574	1,069,424	+3%	54,641	-1%	3,061
1996	255,529	755,296	1,038,853	-3%	58,532	+7%	3,155
1997	304,364	820,359	1,155,803	+11%	59,110	+1%	3,062
1998	303,784	927,534	1,264,327	+9%	64,695	+9%	2,743
1999	314,368	992,289	1,334,073	+6%	63,734	-1%	2,828
2000	358,650	**1,144,595**	**1,523,380**	+14%	64,289	+1%	3,683
2001	397,216	1,132,915	1,550,157	+2%	67,621	+5%	3,293
2002	414,128	1,007,131	1,430,758	-8%	49,125	-27%	2,671
2003	921,532	984,507	1,924,945	+35%	48,590	-1%	3,559
2004	930,987	948,434	1,893,748	-2%	43,022	-11%	2,857
2005	938,977	833,140	1,786,573	-6%	43,026	+0%	2,605
2006	**1,030,761**	969,640	**2,031,489**	+14%	42,009	-2%	2,333
2007	1,091,774	1,007,339	2,116,685	+4%	43,973	+5%	2,423
2008	1,091,078	892,158	1,999,841	-6%	37,125	-16%	1,341
2009	929,386	698,935	1,634,544	-18%	26,992	-27%	191
2010	747,442	653,987	1,408,199	-14%	25,616	-5%	42
2011	296,060	268,199	564,259	-10%	14,405	+24%	446

Notes:

- Total passengers includes transit passengers (one way).
- Statistics are per twelve-month period (calendar year).
- Prior to 1989 statistics do not differentiate charter and scheduled passengers.
- Freight includes freight and mail in metric tonnes.
- Movements are the total number, including air transport, freight, positioning, training, club and other (private, military, etc.).
- Figures for 2011 are for January–June inclusive.

From the 'glory growth days' of the 1980s when holiday charter flights were the airport's mainstay, Air Europe Boeing 737-300 G-BMTH. (Geoff Jones)

INDEX

References to pictures are shown with a (p); 'col' denotes a picture in the plate section.

RECOMMENDED FURTHER READING AND USEFUL WEBSITES

Cronin, Mike, *Doesn't Time Fly? Aer Lingus – Its History*, The Collins Press (2011)
Gaskell, Keith, *British Airways: Its History, Aircraft & Liveries*, Airlife (1999)
Halford-MacLeod, Guy, *Britain's Airlines – Volume 2: 1951–1964*, Tempus (2007)
———, *Volume 3: 1964 to Deregulation*, The History Press (2010)
Jones, Ivor, *Cardiff Airfields*, Aureus Publishing (2003)
———, *Airfields & Landing Grounds of Wales: South*, Tempus (2007)
Marriott, Leo, *British Airports*, Ian Allan (1993)
Merton-Jones, Tony, *British Independent Airlines Since 1946* (4 volumes), LAAS and Merseyside Aviation Society (1976)
Phillips, Alan, *Civil Aviation in Wales*, Bridge Books (2008)
Simons, Graham M., *The Spirit of Dan-Air*, GMS Enterprises (1993)
Smith, David J., *Action Stations 3. – Military Airfields of Wales & the North-West*, Patrick Stephens (1981)
Staddon, T.G., *History of Cambrian Airways 1935–1976*, Airline Publications & Sales Ltd (1979)
Thursby, Robert C., *Eheda – Glamorgan Aviation*, Tempus (2002)

Aeros (Flight School), www.pftraining.co.uk
Cambrian Airways Society, www.cambrianairways.org.uk (Gary Hilliard's website with masses of pictorial, historical and other information about Cambrian Airways)
Cardiff Airport, www.tbicardiffairport.com
Rhoose Flying Club Cafe & Bar, www.rhooseflyingclub.co.uk
Signature Flight Support (BBA Aviation), www.signatureflight.com/locations (search under Wales)
South Wales Aviation Group, http://cardiffandstathan.blogspot.com/ (an excellent and comprehensive site produced by Ian Grinter and colleagues)
Wales Air Network, www.walesairnetwork.com (supporting Wales' air links and infrastructure)